THE FIVE YEAR MARK

MIKE SAUNDERS

Copyright © 2016 by Michael Saunders

All rights reserved. This book or any portion thereof may not be reproduced or used in any manner whatsoever without the express written permission of the publisher, except for the use of brief quotations in a book review.

Printed in South Africa

First Printing, 2016

ISBN-13: 978-1539008781

ISBN-10: 1539008789

Address:

Suite 7, Abrey Eco Park

5 Abrey Road

Kloof

South Africa

www.digitlab.co.za

DEDICATION

To God, who has designed me for more than I expect of myself. You are the ultimate example of influence and leadership.

To my beautiful, ever faithful and supportive wife, Stacey. You are the wind in my sails and the love of my life.

To my son Zac, this is part of my story. I hope it inspires you to, one day, write your own.

HOW TO USE THIS BOOK

This book was written for you in short, easy-to-read chapters.

Each chapter illustrates a particular idea or principle you can apply to your own entrepreneurial or business journey. Feel free to bounce around the chapters as you please or read it from start to finish.

SHARING THIS BOOK

If you would like to share aspects of this book, or encourage an online conversation around it on social media, you are most welcome to. Use the hashtag #FiveYearMark if you can, and feel free to tag me on @mikeasaunders.

If you enjoy this book, it would be great if you could post a review on Amazon. Simply search for my name on Amazon to find my author profile and this book. Thanks a million!

ACKNOWLEDGMENTS

To my wife, Stacey, for making me believe in the pages of this book enough to write it.

To my father, the late Raymond Saunders, who remains a highly influential, yet humble hero.

To Mom, your unwavering support and long list of achievements always inspire me to go further and push harder.

To the best business partners: Frank Smit, Darren Young and Steve Gardner.

To Meegan Rourke-McGill and Paula Barrett, for agreeing to be the first employees of a company that had nothing but a dream.

To my editors, Catherine Jenkin and Elaine Young thank you for seeing the vision for the book and helping me reach it.

Jimmy Wales for a 30-minute conversation that still inspires me. To Bill Hybels, David Novak, John Dickson, Jim Collins and Clayton Cristensen for mentoring me through the pages in your books.

Mike Smallbones and Scripture Union for risking with me on my first leadership assignment. Keith Coats for unlocking potential in me and so many others.

The people and clients of DigitLab, past and present. Thank you for everything you have done to unlock a dream. To the best business coaches I know, Brent "Spillly" Spilkin and Graham Kiggan.

To Jude Foulston, for starting this whole thing. Over coffee, you helped me get excited about writing the book that lives in my heart. Finally, to everyone who reads this, thanks for taking the time to learn about our journey. I hope it helps you with your own.

CONTENTS

Foreword by Keith Coats
Introduction

LEARNING TO DREAM

Be Brave
Dream Big
Failure is Part of Success
Position Yourself
Give Back to the Industry

LEADING PEOPLE

Unlock Potential Within People
Narrative Over Vision
Helping People Win
Clarity is King
People Need a Challenge
Why we Don't Delegate

MIKE SAUNDERS

THE NUTS AND BOLTS OF OUR BUSINESS

Masters of Excellence

(1+1)>2

Chart Your Own Course

Cash Helps You Breathe

Focus on Output

Never Pitch Over the Phone

Play the End Game

Work on the Business

Build for Sale

CULTURE

The Small Wins

Recruit the Right People

Autonomy and Trust

#workfamily

Have Fun

FIVE YEAR MARK

PERSONAL DEVELOPMENT

Know Thyself
Integrity is Everything
Be Humble
Learn to Take Criticism
The Tough Conversations
Dealing With Stress
Eggs in One Basket

PLANNING THE NEXT FIVE

Be Willing to Change
Dream Big…Again

MIKE SAUNDERS

FOREWORD

BY KEITH COATS

Mike Saunders is one of those rare individuals we all admire. He knows what he is chasing; yet he seems to find the time to pause and enjoy life. He is confident in his abilities, but always remains open to learning. He is not afraid of taking risks; yet he has the capacity to 'take others along with him'.

I first met Mike at the request of a mutual friend who explained that Mike was looking to pursue a new direction, and thought I might be of some assistance. I agreed and, soon after meeting Mike, I realised that there was much he could teach me. I offered to drink repeated cups of coffee with him, letting him gain whatever benefits he might accrue as a result, in exchange for his mentoring me in the ways of social media. I remain convinced that I was the major beneficiary of this arrangement that, aside from the consumption of countless cups of coffee, precipitated the growth of a friendship.

Mike started DigitLab and became an Associate of TomorrowToday. The latter role was relinquished when it became obvious that DigitLab required his full attention and focus. During that time, I watched Mike deal with some difficult personal circumstances and emerge stronger, wiser and better for having gone through such tough times. I have seen his business flourish and marvelled at his unbridled enthusiasm, no matter what the challenges or circumstances.

Mike is one of those people who shape the future. He knows his stuff and is seemingly always that 'one step ahead' of everyone else. This can cause trouble on occasion, but is the very essence of a good entrepreneur – something that Mike undoubtedly is! This book is an important and significant marker in Mike's journey, because it represents something smart leaders do – taking time to reflect and to pause. The process of writing this book has been a gift to Mike as much as it will be a real benefit to all who read it.

Mike has achieved a great deal and learnt much along the way. This book is a reflection of that, but it is only a marker in what promises to be an interesting journey to come. As a result of reading this book, I am certain you will feel inspired to aim higher, think deeper and not be afraid to give it a go. That is what Mike did and continues to do. I, for one, look forward to reading the next instalment…

FIVE YEAR MARK

1

INTRODUCTION

It's been said that the first five years of business are the toughest. Apparently, five out of seven small businesses started in South Africa will fold within their first year of operation (Sowetan Live, 2016). Aspirant and existing entrepreneurs face huge challenges and frustrations in South Africa (702, 2016) and need to find ways to develop sustainable businesses that build the local economy. Entrepreneurship may not be easy, but it is the most rewarding work I have ever done.

Why would I write a book at such an early stage in our business? This is not a story of building Google, revolutionising the mobile industry like Steve Jobs or starting a social media revolution like Twitter did. It's the story of a young entrepreneur who was inspired by these great digital revolutions. It's my story, as I set out to build a business in the digital industry. I have had a few successes over the years but I have not even come close to achieving the dream I hope to unlock in this lifetime.

Steven Fry said in his show "Steven Fry Live: More Fool Me" that, as he got older, he was more able to look back on his younger self as if he were another person. He writes books as if writing to his younger self – his first book was the book he wished he could have read when he was young.

In many ways, this book is something I wish I could have read during the early years of my entrepreneurial journey. It would have saved me some time and money, and perhaps I would be further along the way to entrepreneurial success than I am today.

Over the years I read many books, listened to many podcasts and watched hundreds of TED Talks which were all interesting, and most added some value to my journey. The lessons I learnt were from people who had walked similar journeys to the one I wished to walk. They were inspiring, but often they lacked practical teaching and advice. I could not see how to apply these lessons to my smaller world. Until I read "Axiom".

"Axiom", penned by Bill Hybels, is one of the most useful books I have ever read. It's a book of short chapters, each of which simply explains the lessons Bill learnt during his journey, through which he built one of the most globally renowned churches. I have re-read "Axiom" numerous times and shared what I have learnt from it with many people. I enjoyed the book so much, because it made simple what I sometimes saw as difficult or complex. "Axiom" helped me learn from Bill's mistakes, instead of making my own. In a way I feel it helped me skip a few years of learning so that I could become a more effective leader.

That's why I wrote this book – to do the same thing for others. Through "The Five Year Mark", I'm sharing my journey, the lessons I've learnt and the stories behind the company I started five years ago.

I believe that entrepreneurship is one of the most powerful solutions to poverty. I also believe that I am not on this earth simply to start a business; I'm also here to help as many people as possible start and grow their own businesses. That's exactly what we do at DigitLab – we use digital business practices and marketing techniques to grow people's businesses. In turn, they hire more people, add more value and generate a stronger economy. I have purposefully over-simplified the concept but I believe it's true: entrepreneurship adds true value to people's lives, the economy and society.

DigitLab turned five in February 2016. We have made it this far – they've been difficult, but exhilarating years. I have loved building DigitLab into what it is today and I love seeing what it has become. The people I have met and been able to work with along the way, have inspired me. I have enjoyed the successes and pushed through the times I felt like giving up. I have put my heart, soul and mind into building this company. I love that my dream is coming true and I only hope that this book helps someone to see his or her dreams through. I want this to be an "Axiom" for someone who reads it.

There's no better feeling than looking back and seeing it all come together – when everything you hoped for, every dream you had, is coming true and all that hard work is paying off.

I've been privileged to live this entrepreneurial journey, and it's thanks to the sharing of learning, advice and mentorship that I've got this far. I hope that this book is one that helps you build and grow your business to…The Five Year Mark.

FIVE YEAR MARK

LEARNING TO DREAM

"If you can dream it, you can do it"
Walt Disney

MIKE SAUNDERS

2

BE BRAVE

Bruce, a good friend and mentor of mine, once shared a story with me of his army days in the 1970s. After boarding an overnight civilian passenger train, he fell asleep in his compartment. At two o'clock in the morning, Bruce dreamt that the train was about to propel itself over a cliff. In his sleep, he reacted by jumping up, and he 'sleep ran' down the passage, away from the direction of travel, to an exit door. That's where he stopped and hesitated. The train was travelling at high speed. Then, still believing it was doomed, he tentatively 'jumped' out, not letting go of the chrome handrail. He woke up as his feet hit the stones around the railway sleepers and managed to pull himself on board again. Needless to say, his feet were torn up, his body was pumping with adrenaline and he was crying like a good soldier.

Bruce's dream gave him a very different sense of reality, causing him to act quickly so that he could change his understanding of the norm: nobody wants to sit on a train that's driving off a cliff.

Some people dream about a better world; a better way of doing things; a simpler life; excellence in a field of work; or just about anything that is different from today's norm. They dream about a future that doesn't exist yet and begin to hope that they can be a part of it, or help create it

Dreams have been the starting point of the abolition of slavery, the beginning of companies like Apple and Google, and the reason people give up everything to pursue a greater cause. Dreams are powerful and, in the right hands, they can change the world we live in.

A dream is often an end point – a picture of what's possible. Dreams are inspirational, utopian and seem real enough that they could be possible. In fact, dreams taunt us into believing that they *are* possible. Dreams can unlock your potential or they can grip you with fear – a fear that you'll never be what you thought you could be.

Dreams are an enigma. They can be dangerous, risky and difficult to achieve – but they dangle the hope of a better life, improved experience or even the creation of a better world. Although not everyone understands dreams, people all over the world pursue them.

Many people choose not to follow their dreams.

FIVE YEAR MARK

I believe they choose not to, because of the gap that exists between the norm and their dream. They can't stomach the thought of the work, the risk or the pain they might experience if they chase their particular dream.

A year ago, I was sitting in a coffee shop and an acquaintance spotted me. He settled down for a quick chat, and he knew that I ran my own business. He enquired about our progress as a company, and I gave him a brief overview of what we've been up to and what our plans are.

He then started telling me about the business idea that he was itching to pursue. It was his dream. He highlighted how fantastic an idea it was, how the target market exists for it, and then he told me about the client who was ready to sign.

I asked him the question that is fast becoming my standard response in this situation: "What are you waiting for, why haven't you started it yet?" I've had many conversations like that and, nearly every time, they end with a statement like: "We just need to fill these gaps and then we'll begin".

Here's the hard truth: the gaps are always there; the right client is missing; the right team is not yet complete; the product hasn't been developed yet; the current job is too comfortable; or the Moon appears to be in the wrong position. Bruce didn't wait to get dressed before he decided to take action to save his life – he figured he'd work the rest out once he had jumped off the death train.

Dreaming about an entrepreneurial life will never materialise until you decide that your dream is more important than all the gaps. It's tough jumping into something where your future seems unclear – but you should, at the least, trust that you or your team can overcome the obstacles within it, no matter what.

A personal dream of mine has always been marriage and family. I love the idea of a big family filled with love, happiness and support. When I sat at the precipice of my second marriage in May 2015, all the usual questions came to mind: Do we have the stamina to make this marriage work? Will we be great parents? Will we be able to have children? What happens if my business fails? What if I can't support our family and way of life? Will she resent me? Will she support me?

There are always going to be so many questions and so many gaps. In marriage, you don't commit because you've ironed out all the gaps. You get married because being married to the person you love is more important than the gaps. You trust yourself and your future spouse and believe that, no matter what you hit, you will work it out and find a way.

FIVE YEAR MARK

Starting a business is exactly the same: you need to believe your idea is worth pursuing and that, no matter what gaps and challenges you face, you're in it for the long haul. Start the business, put your head down and find a way to make it work. Otherwise, you will never realise the dream set on your heart.

DigitLab began as a dream to see people connect through technology. We decided that creating a digital agency was the best way to see this happen. We wanted to work with businesses, marketers, innovators and anyone who is looking to create more meaningful connections with people. The dream behind DigitLab was full of gaps when we started. Moreover, I firmly believe that our team is – only now – complete, after five years. Between day one of operations and today, we've been solving problems as they come our way, and doing it the best way we know how.

We have found people who believe in us, people who trust us and people who care about our success. This has been our journey. We did not have it all worked out before we began, but we were clear about what we needed to do to start seeing our dream come true.

Simply, if you are not brave enough to pursue your dream, if it doesn't mean that much to you, you will never see that dream come true.

3

FAILURE IS PART OF SUCCESS

A few years ago, I arrived in Lagos to present at a conference. It was my first trip to Nigeria and I was nervously excited to represent DigitLab in a new country and explore the opportunities Nigeria had to offer.

As I arrived, I stood in the longest airport queue I have ever been in and quickly noticed there was no air-conditioning. There's nothing like standing in a long, sweaty queue, without cellphone signal, in the middle of Africa, unable to go anywhere, to remind you just how small you actually are! Brene Brown once said that, when we lack an answer to a situation or problem, we naturally make up our own story. Often, the story we make up is a lot worse than reality. Because we lacked an explanation for why the queue was taking so long, we began coming up with pretty creative stories which included politics, jail and missing person reports. Of course, we all began to get a bit skittish about what would happen next.

FIVE YEAR MARK

After waiting for what felt like another hour, I made it past border control and headed towards the collection point, carefully scanning all the hospitality boards to find my host for the trip.

I was relieved when a very professional, yet very friendly, man met me and guided me to the baggage collection point. At that time, Nigeria was constructing their airport buildings and facilities, so the baggage collection point was guarded by the largest, strongest, meanest-looking nightclub bouncer sort, standing over a pile of suitcases that had been taken off the aeroplane.

All I had to do was show my boarding pass stub and he would give me my bag – a very simple process, unless of course you no longer have your boarding stub.

I had somehow lost my stub between the aeroplane and the baggage point. I began to feel quite stressed, especially because the bouncer was now yelling at me in a language that was clearly not my mother tongue. Nigerians are the most wonderful people, with loudly passionate communication skills. This is one of the things I love most about them, but at first introduction, all this passionate yelling was enough to make me believe my life was over.

Thankfully, my host engaged in an epic battle of words and managed to get the bouncer to release my bag. I began to think all this chaos would be over soon.

No such luck. An equally frightening, bodyguard-looking gentleman approached me and asked for my Yellow Card. I proudly presented him with the documents that I had managed to arrange that morning, back in South Africa.

Of course, you're here for the drama right now, and I'm about to deliver it. When entering Nigeria, your Yellow Card or immunisation certificate needs to have been valid for a few months before you can be permitted to visit the country. Mine wasn't. Thankfully, after another battle of tongues that my host engaged in on my behalf, I was released and we were able to make our way out of the airport. At this point, I was struggling to look calm, mainly because I was not – I was anything but. In fact, I had already begun making my peace with destiny and imagining how I'd miss everyone back home because I'd never see them again. I was not operating within a rational frame of mind at all.

We headed out of the airport, where I'd expected a car to be outside, waiting to collect me. Instead, I was guided to a rather dingy-looking parking lot, and quickly found myself in front of a white minibus with tinted windows. It was at this point that I had my final conversation with my Creator.

Just then, the door slid open and, to my surprise, sitting in the van and catching up on email was Jimmy Wales, the co-founder of Wikipedia, looking as cool as ice.

FIVE YEAR MARK

Suddenly all my nervousness faded as I tried my best not to look too much like a fan boy in front of this incredible Internet legend.

The ride to the hotel was surreal. I enjoyed half an hour of picking Jimmy's brain about various things related to the Internet and social media. I listened intently as he told me the story of starting Nupedia (Wikipedia's predecessor) and how it hadn't worked out. Jimmy told me that it had taught him a lot about what he needed to make Wikipedia succeed, sharing with me the value of community and collaboration. That half hour has by far been one of my favourite half hours ever experienced in business.

Jimmy's story is not unique. Every entrepreneur I know has experienced at least one failure in their past. In fact, failure has now become something that business investors look for in entrepreneurs before they are willing to invest. When we launched Monocle (our real-time social intelligence tool) to the market, we met with business investors to get their thoughts about its potential for success. Every single investor and mentor asked about our company's previous failures, to assess how much we had learnt and could apply to this new venture.

Failure proves you have cut your teeth, you've learnt valuable lessons, and that you're able to get past the tough times. Failure proves that you are willing and committed to reinventing – rebuilding, redesigning and re-creating anything you need to, in order to succeed.

My first failed business taught me that marketing and sales are essential for business success. It also taught me that you must partner with people you trust. My second failed business taught me that industry solutions must be affordable for the market they're being sold to. It also taught me about finding the right name, when a large international media house threatened to sue me for trademark infringement unless I shut my business down. My third business was not a failure, but I decided to sell my shares and leave the business, because I learnt that I only have a certain number of hours in the day and I needed to put my energy into what mattered most.

All of my failures in business have made me less concerned about failing. Failure just means we're trying, that we're pushing the boundaries, that we're not happy with the current state of things, and that we believe we can do more. Each time we fail, we learn. Each time we learn, we get better, sharper and smarter. Failure in business doesn't mean *you're* a failure – you are only a failure when you stop trying.

4

POSITION YOURSELF

Positioning yourself within a market is one of the most important aspects of business. Most people chalk it up to a marketing exercise, but I have found the practice of positioning to be far more powerful and important. Positioning yourself correctly within your market is a vital business strategy for entrepreneurs. It's a strategy that helps you mould the business you hope to build and still earn a living.

The process of positioning also helped me dig into why I had started my company. I'd always had a small issue with going into business on my own. While I knew that every business needed to be profitable, I loathed the idea of constantly chasing the next deal and living for turnover and profit ratios. I needed to know that we were doing something more valuable, that we were chasing a better purpose. I needed to know that I would be able to use our profitability as a tool to solve some of the injustice I saw in the world.

The first injustice I wanted to put right, was that people are exploited at work. Most businesses that I'd worked for didn't trust or value their employees. They didn't unlock their true potential. They saw employees as workhorses or machines instead of partners.

This was evident in the way they resourced, trusted and challenged their staff. I wanted to change that. I wanted to build a business that trusted the people we hired, that supported them, and that was known for getting the best out of people.

The second injustice I wanted to address was more of a passion than an injustice. I am inspired and intrigued by the ways in which technology can bring people closer to each other. I wanted to help people see the value of technology and how it improves human life. I wanted to work with a team of people that was committed to helping people succeed in a digital world.

It's important to know why you are in business – what you are trying to solve, change or be. It's important because it will frame every conversation and challenge you face in business.

FIVE YEAR MARK

The best positioning exercise I have discovered comes from the former Head of Marketing and Communications at Google, Christopher Escher. I appreciate his method because it's so simple – you can have a positioning statement within a few minutes. This is how it works:

- For (target customer);
- Who (statement of need or opportunity);
- (Product name) is a (product category);
- That (statement of key benefit);
- Unlike (competing alternative);
- (Product name) (statement of primary differentiation).

When I applied this to DigitLab, I ended up with this:

"DigitLab is for marketing professionals and entrepreneurs who need to take the next progressive step in digital. DigitLab is a digital agency that believes in the power of digital to bring people closer to brands, businesses and each other. Unlike many businesses, DigitLab will encourage and trust its people to add value to the organisation."

Positioning DigitLab in this light meant that I now had a business idea that replicated my belief system. It meant that I knew what success looked like. I was excited.

This exercise began to shape my plan for business growth. In essence, I found it easier to find and attract people who had problems like the one I was solving.

When marketing DigitLab, I used a simple marketing technique called Inbound Marketing. Inbound marketing suggests that if you create content online that appeals to your target market, you can use that content to draw your target market closer to your business. This ultimately results in a sale.

My first year as a social media consultant, the year before we started DigitLab, was a tough year. I had seen that companies were struggling with how to apply social media to their marketing plans. I set out to solve the problem by enabling people to develop their skills in implementing social media strategies. I provided training sessions for people wanting to learn more. I ended up working almost 100 hours per week so that I could meet potential clients, close deals, do the actual work and still learn as much about the industry as I could.

Needless to say, I was running out of time in my day to action any marketing strategy for myself. I needed to find a way to attract people and businesses looking to progress their marketing plans into the social media space.

I opted to streamline my learning and marketing exercises. I read every article, book and paper I could on social media and compiled what I had learnt into 500-word articles. I then posted these articles on my blog. I found that the process of writing a blog post about a social media concept forced me to understand, in detail, how that concept worked. This process reinforced my learning and helped me get more out of my time. It also showed anyone who read that blog that I understood social media, and it initiated many conversations with people that eventually became clients.

Blogging has a not-so-hidden secret, in that it helps you build your profile in search engines. The more you blog, the better your search engine results placement. I began to enjoy some prime placement in search results when people searched for 'social media'.

Of course, word of mouth is everything, and that's why my first few clients came to me through personal connections – people I knew, who referred me to others who needed my help. Over time, I started to get a steady stream of meeting requests coming through my blog. The most interesting one came about four months after I started blogging.

In 2009, I received a call from the South African Presidency. They were looking for a social media consultant to advise the Presidency on the next steps towards developing their social media presence. I agreed to a consultation and presented an education proposal, which was never accepted. Although I did not land a big contract in this story, I learnt a big lesson on positioning. When I got the call, I asked the lady on the phone how she had heard about me. She said she had been searching online for 'social media' and found my blog. She said that, as far as she could work out, I was the best social media consultant in South Africa.

Let me be very clear on this one: I was, by no means, the best social media consultant in South Africa. There were a lot of very smart people working in social media at the time and they were doing some really fantastic work. The key here is that, somehow, within four months of working for myself, I had found myself positioned as a key player in the South African social media industry.

Later that year, I had another interesting phone call, where someone I'd never met asked me to speak at a conference. All they said was: "I have read your blogs and listened to your podcasts. I just need to know what you charge and if you are free on the 23rd February." The content I was producing online was being consumed and it was becoming a very successful marketing and sales pipeline.

The very same year, I was approached by a prominent social media agency to open their Durban office. They were impressed by my presence in the industry. Another advertising agency in Durban approached me and suggested we start a digital agency. Each of these engagements came about because people believed that I knew what I was talking about and saw me as a key player in the industry.

My blog became a catalogue of content, sharing my passion with avid readers. The more I spoke about how the digital world could be used to bring people together, the more people were standing up to take notice. Moreover, they were taking notice of my abilities and potential. Being clear about our position helped show the market what we were about, and this naturally turned into business.

Recently, I was talking to a very talented young person. We were discussing the possibility of her joining our DigitLab team, but I didn't have a position that suited her.

I really wanted her to join our team and I told her this. Her words to me were a clear sign we were getting the second part of our positioning right. She told me she'd love to work for us because:

"Word on the street is that you look after your people."

I was blown away. Finally we had firm evidence that people could see we were different by the way we treated people. Being clear on our position has helped us build a business that people want to work in, resulting in a great team of very talented people helping solve problems for our clients.

The positioning exercise I detailed above is a useful tool, but I have a few additions to it:

Know who you are

I have spent a good part of my life playing in rock bands, and during that time I have met a lot of vocalists desperately trying to sing like Dave Grohl of the Foo Fighters. It's completely understandable: Dave is an incredibly gifted vocalist and he has a very distinct sound. So many rock bands have a front man doing his best to make his voice sound deeper, grittier and edgier than everyone else. It's quite an amusing sight to hear a person's vocal cords straining under the pressure, often combined with a very red-faced singer looking like he is in over his head.

Singing like Dave Grohl, when you're not Dave Grohl, can seriously damage your vocal cords.

I went through a phase of wanting to sing just like Chester Bennington from Linkin Park. I'd do my best to scream in tune and attempt to recreate his vocal talents. Each time, my voice would be ruined for a day afterwards. It took a little time, but I finally accepted that my voice was my voice, and that I should play to its strengths instead of trying to sound like someone I'm not.

It's the same in business. We often spend time trying to be the next Steve Jobs or Richard Branson. But we've forgotten that what made these entrepreneurs so incredible, was that they remained true to themselves.

We don't need to copy their style. We need to find our own style, identify our strengths and enhance them. In business, the best way to position yourself within the market will become clearly apparent when you find out exactly who you are.

Knowing exactly who you are is the most important aspect of positioning, but it's not always that simple. Who you are in business involves your value structure, your service, your products, your employees and your future planning.

Know your values

Your values determine who you will work with and why. It's important to know this as early as possible in your entrepreneurial journey. If you wait, you may end up taking on work you don't actually want. Values create a fundamental rulebook that helps you see when your boundaries are being overstepped. Knowing your values and learning to articulate them will help you to know when they are being challenged. In our business we have core values that are agreed upon and discussed by all our directors. Our values dictate the kind of business and people we hope to be.

It has taken some time to articulate our values, but it's been worth every minute.

When we first started DigitLab, we couldn't articulate our values in simple words or statements, so we discussed ways to identify when we might be getting close to crossing a value-based line. Then we agreed that if we ever got close to this line, we would meet to discuss a way forward. When starting a business, it's not always easy to find the right words to explain how and why you do business, so we found this tactic useful in starting the right conversations before it was too late.

Find clients who need you

Your service offering is often designed around your client or customers. We live in a customer-centric world, but entrepreneurs need to do more than just meet a client's needs. We need to find clients who require the services or product we've designed, so that they can build their businesses. If clients need what you have put onto the market, 80% of the battle for customer-centricity is won.

We also need to encourage clients to take the next step, to explore new options and to build their business even more. Our role as business owners is to build our business to deliver on the current needs of our clients, while keeping a good eye on their future needs. These future needs will help us to build our business so that it remains relevant tomorrow.

Essentially, we built a service offering we believed in and then went out to find people who needed those services. If they asked for or needed something outside of our domain, we would refer the client to recommended service providers. One of the biggest elements of deciding what you do for your clients lies in deciding what you don't do.

Knowing who you want to be will have a profound impact on the future planning of your business. I know that I love pioneering new ideas – it's something I love most about DigitLab. Understanding this has meant that I set out to attract a team of committed, talented and capable people who want to run projects and divisions once I have finished setting them up. Which brings me to my next point.

Hire accordingly

For us, hiring was a simple task. I knew what we were building, so it was easy to know who to hire next and what kind of people we were looking for. I always hired people who were better at the job than me. While I may be a 'Jack of all trades', a business needs specialists to create divisions and run projects. This, in turn, creates and builds a better, stronger and more robust business.

The people on the DigitLab team are much smarter than I am in their fields – this has been the most important part of DigitLab. As a collective, we are much stronger than any individual.

Our hiring process is two-fold. We first assess and analyse competency levels. Potential candidates undergo a series of tests and interviews to ensure that they are the best person to do the job. If they're successful in these, they move on to meeting me for one final interview.

We call this the culture interview. I don't ask candidates about their abilities or skills. In this interview, I dig into their lives to better understand what makes them tick. I learn about their passions, their dreams and aspirations. Essentially, I look to see how they fit into our business and if we, as a company, can help their dreams come true. If we fit well together, they're hired.

Market what you want to do

Entrepreneurs regularly face this problem: we know what we want to do, but we haven't done it yet. The big compromise is that we choose to do things we don't want to do because they pay the bills, and we do these while waiting for the client or investor that buys into the work we truly want to do.

FIVE YEAR MARK

The trouble with this philosophy is that we become known for what we do, not for what we want to do. We start getting more opportunities to do the work we don't want to do, instead of the work we do want to do.

As a new business owner, I admit we've taken on work we're capable of, but it hasn't been our core business offering. Sometimes it helps with solving cash flow problems, and occasionally that's unavoidable. We do choose, however, not to promote this work. We don't share or talk about it, and we don't use it as a marketing tool. It's not that we're not proud of it, because our team will always commit to creating the best possible work. It's just that we don't want to be known for this type of work.

If we couldn't find clients that wanted to hire us to do the work we loved, we started talking about that kind of work more. We would write about the possibilities or we would run test projects that became case studies that we used as marketing tools. We even did work for clients at cost, so that we could show people what we were passionate about doing. In a sense, we built our portfolio of work exactly around the work we wanted to do, not just the work we had to do.

Entrepreneurs must ensure that the world, and the market they want to serve, sees and understands them clearly and correctly: doing the things they are passionate about instead of the things that they have no passion for.

5

GIVE BACK TO THE INDUSTRY

I'm writing this chapter whilst in transit between Dubai and Singapore. Ed Sheeran is keeping me company while I type, as I'm watching his Wembley Live Concert.

Ed Sheeran is a master performance artist. He uses simplicity as an attraction technique – it's just him, his guitar and 80 000 people in the audience. It's a simplicity that works though, as every member of that audience is paying rapt attention to his every word. Then he spins out the magic and brings Elton John on stage to join him for a duet performance of "Don't Go Breaking My Heart".

Collaborations are something we see a lot of in music. Great musicians are always looking for new people to collaborate with; they find reasons to perform together, to write together and to promote the music industry together. Great musicians are more interested in making music than self-promotion. They realise that collaboration helps them meet new audiences, enables them to grow musically, networks them into the industry better, and creates a much more magical product for the fans.

We need to find ways to bring this magic of collaboration to our business world. We need to embrace collaboration and knowledge-sharing so that we can create a much better product for our customers. In our digital industry, we tend to share a lot of information online and, while this looks like knowledge-sharing, it's more of a marketing activity. We need to focus on true collaboration, to accelerate the learning and development of expertise in our industry.

Any and every industry can benefit from industry players putting their pride aside and starting initiatives that promote the growth and acceleration of their own industries. Initiatives like Cerebra's 27dinners and World Wide Creative's Heavy Chef Sessions, inspired us to start something like them in our very own city, Durban.

Our CTO at DigitLab, Steve, told me how he wanted to start the Durban chapter of a Mobile Meetup. Mobile Meetups are a collaborative exercise, with a mobile platform called Appcelerator, which seek to build knowledge and skills within the mobile development industry.

During our discussion, we saw a huge opportunity for networking with local mobile developers and accelerating our learning in a field that was clouded with many opinions and development options. We picked a date, rented some chairs and kitted out the empty office across the hallway with your normal event paraphernalia. It was a small event, but something really unexpected began to happen – something I could not have anticipated.

The mobile development industry in Durban started to work together. Normally, competitors hold onto every inch of their intellectual property. But thanks to our Mobile Meetup, developers started to share code structures, work flows, preferred platforms, user experience ideas and a wide range of personal experiences.

That evening, I started to see that events like this are the equivalent of concerts in the music industry. These events accelerate industry understanding, expertise and experience. They inspire and invigorate people, and those people start energising the industry. These events promote the industry to clients, help to generate revenue, develop new products and produce content. They build collective traction for an industry, which ultimately benefits everyone who works within it, or uses it for their business.

After a few Mobile Meetup events we saw the audience changing from developers to marketers and digital experts. That's when we decided to reinvent the idea.

At the beginning of 2015, we launched Digital Swarm. Digital Swarm exists as a platform for sharing ideas across the broad spectrum of Digital Business and Marketing. We wanted to see the entire Durban industry collaborating in the same way we saw the development community collaborating. We also wanted to create something that possessed potential for global expansion, so that it fit with our own company's vision for international expansion.

Digital Swarm has become a vehicle that provides DigitLab with an opportunity to host some great speakers from local and international agencies. Digital Swarm has helped us forge new relationships that make us a stronger agency.

I am committed to spending time giving back to the industry we work in, and here's why:

You'll give your vision legs

When you plug your resources into building the industry, you are able to give your dream stronger and faster legs. It becomes easier to find like-minded people, convince others of your vision and ultimately inspire more people to see your dream through. Your vision and reason for being in business have a bigger chance of being embedded into the fabric of the industry.

You'll build rapport

Giving back to the industry builds trust with the stakeholders in your industry. You'll build a relationship of trust with potential partners, clients, governing bodies, legislative associations and potential talent.

You'll attract people you can learn from

This was the unexpected win for me. As we committed to Digital Swarm and it gained traction, we found that we were able to attract better talent and expertise to the event – people that I was excited to learn from and grow with. Our aim with Digital Swarm was never to put ourselves on the platform. We are the hosts, not the experts. Ultimately, the more experts we could find to share their experiences through our platform, the more we were growing.

Experts are busy people though, and they tend to look for good platforms to speak from. As we developed our small event and built a loyal community, we found that experts were more open to speaking at our event, which benefitted both the expert speaker and the Digital Swarm community.

I put this to the test in Singapore, at a conference I attended. A prominent Google thought leader was speaking at the event and I managed to catch him for a few minutes in the speakers' lounge. I learnt a bit about what he was doing and told him about Digital Swarm. I asked if he'd be open to conducting a quick Google Hangout recorded interview about a new product Google was launching. He agreed. It was humbling to know that he was open to helping us build a digital community, and a massive privilege to host such a big digital heavyweight at our Digital Swarm.

MIKE SAUNDERS

FIVE YEAR MARK

LEADING PEOPLE

"A leader is a dealer in hope"
Napoleon Bonaparte

MIKE SAUNDERS

6

UNLOCK POTENTIAL WITHIN PEOPLE

Every person on the face of the planet has potential. The potential within people is what led to the construction of the Great Wall of China, Europe's captivating and incredible architecture, and the creation of the Internet. Potential is what resided within Simone Biles, the Olympic gold medalist, when she first stepped onto the gymnastics platform.

Potential lives in the gap between who you are today and who you could be in the future. Potential looks beyond your current abilities and today's circumstances. Potential looks towards a future version of yourself and challenges you to progress.

As leaders, our primary objective should be to unlock the potential within others. We should be dedicating vast amounts of our time to understanding our people and figuring out how to reach that untapped magic. It's through that process that your team will grow and, by default, your business too. It's not always easy to see your own potential. We tend to be too limited by our individual perception of circumstances, abilities and opportunities. That's why we often need other people to show us our own potential and, if we're lucky, help us to unlock it.

As a leader, I need to look for the potential within people and help them unlock it. I count this as one of the best parts of my job, because in my own life I have reaped tremendous benefits from people taking the time to unlock the potential within me.

Meeting with Keith Coats was, for me, an excellent example of this. Keith was the founder of an incredibly well reputed futurist-consulting firm, TomorrowToday, and I was eager to learn from him. I'd asked to meet Keith because I wanted his advice on setting up a successful consulting firm, which was what I was planning to do next in my career.

While we were talking, I was a bit taken aback because Keith seemed far more interested in hearing about my work, than telling me about his. That's when Keith put a crazy proposal on the table. He asked me to mentor him! I was shocked to hear this, but taking advantage of my stunned silence, Keith explained:

It's called reverse mentorship. Reverse mentorship takes place when an experienced businessperson mentors a younger businessperson and, in turn, the younger person mentors the older or more experienced person in the use of new social technologies.

It made sense – all I had to do was teach Keith what I knew about social media and he would teach me what he knew about starting a consultancy.

Keith saw potential within me that I couldn't see. I was so busy looking for what I thought I needed that I couldn't see the value I could already bring. Keith saw more potential within me than I saw in myself. He believed in me more than I did – something that became hugely motivational for me. I lived off that motivation for years, knowing that I was doing something valuable because Keith could see how valuable it was.

It was only a few years later that I saw the genius in the reverse mentorship programme Keith suggested. By asking me to contribute to his growth, Keith spoke to a number of motivating factors that inspired me:

- He recognised the value I could bring;
- He gave me the responsibility to coach him;
- He gave me a sense of achievement;
- He provided me with my very first opportunity to work with a consulting client; and
- He gave me a chance to test my capacity to grow.

Keith was attempting to motivate me towards unlocking my own potential, and it worked. The most difficult part of this process is that you can't do the work for the person – you can only motivate and inspire them.

How can we motivate our team more within our business? Keith's approach speaks to Fredrick Hertzberg's model of motivation. Hertzberg suggests people are not motivated by *hygiene factors* in their work environment.

Hygiene factors are listed as:

- Compensation
- Job security
- Organisational politics
- Working conditions
- Quality of leadership
- Relationships

Hygiene factors need to be fulfilled to ensure people are satisfied with their jobs. However, hygiene factors like these are not motivational tools. Herzberg suggests that people can be motivated and satisfied at work; demotivated and satisfied at work; and motivated but dissatisfied at work. Job satisfaction and motivation are not linked to each other. Trying to motivate people with hygiene factors will lead to better job satisfaction, but not necessarily a more motivated employee or team member.

According to Hertzberg, motivated people are driven by a different list of factors:

- Responsibility
- Job satisfaction
- Recognition
- Achievement
- Opportunities
- Advancement

When looking at unlocking potential within people, we should design careers, projects, job descriptions, mentoring programmes and anything else that person does in ways that:

Make them responsible for outcomes

When we first started DigitLab, we had no choice but to trust people to do their job. It was impossible to check everything, test everything and still get everything done. During those times, we had a very motivated and positive culture at DigitLab.

Then we fell into a trap. One or two people let us down and we started to lose trust in people. We implemented strict work-checking procedures. It sounded like a good plan at first, until we started to see the impact on our culture. Slowly, people stopped taking ownership of projects; they deferred mistakes or problems on to others and became more and more demotivated.

We needed to fix this. According to Hertzberg's model, the problem lay in the fact that we had removed people's responsibility. We needed to change our tactic of protecting people from failure through our work-checking procedures and rather, when people failed, we needed to encourage and trust them to improve from the experience. We cannot expect people to reach their potential if we constantly protect them from failure.

Ensure the hygiene factors are met

Make sure your team is earning a fair and market-related salary. Invest in your leadership by constantly working to improve their ability to lead. Create a stable environment and look after the people in your team.

As a small team, these should be easy to achieve, but as you grow, don't lose sight of the hygiene factors. They are an important foundation for keeping your team motivated.

Recognises the person for the work they do

Recognition should be clear and public. People who contribute something to your team want others to know that they add value to it. It's not enough to be quietly congratulated – we need to take the time to make it public.

Enables them to achieve their goals

David Novak talks in "Taking People with You" about creating hope in people, towards achieving a goal.

As leaders, we have a responsibility to instil hope that the dreams and goals set before people are achievable. David presents these mechanisms to help instil hope in people:

Start with your successes

I was preparing to present our budget to the team for the following year. It was a tough budget to meet because we had to recover from a loss in the previous year. I knew it would be hard to motivate the team after such a difficult year.

I chose to present our budget by showing the team how well we had performed in the previous years, prior to our bad year. Previously, we had doubled the size of the business year on year, and it was extraordinary to see what the team had achieved within the first three years of our business. I reminded them of what we had already done and what we had proven we were capable of. Then I unpacked why we had made a loss in the last year. I needed to do this so that people could plainly see what we had done wrong and what we were changing for the next year.

Using past successes, combined with a good analysis of our failure, we went into the next year believing that it was possible to turn this ship around. We stuck to our belief and, a year later, I was proud to present the good news of a decent profit line.

Look for examples

Sometimes the goals ahead of you are not things you've faced before. In these instances it can be helpful to show how other people and businesses achieved things.

Believe it yourself

You have to believe something is possible yourself. Sometimes though, even leaders start to question the possibility of what they have taken on. If you feel your hope waning, you need to find a way to reinstate the faith and hope you have.

That's where business coaches and mentors can help. It's normal to lose faith every now and then – it's called a 'crisis of belief'. You may experience this crisis when the odds are stacked against you and when things are tough enough to make you question yourself.

It's at these points that we need to dig deep as leaders to find and realise our own leadership potential. More often than not, these moments will help you build a stronger belief in your vision.

My only suggestion here is not to drag your team through your crisis of belief. Rather, work with people you trust in a safe environment as you reinstate your belief in your dream.

Enable people to see the opportunity and advance with it

When Keith presented his reverse mentoring project to me, it created a big opportunity for me to develop a social media training programme and get direct, honest feedback. I knew that if I could successfully develop a programme that worked for Keith, there would be more executives looking for a similar solution. That opportunity helped me to develop one of my first consulting products that I took to market.

A few years later, I was working with someone who eventually left DigitLab. I spent hours trying to inspire him to unlock his personal potential, but he simply could not see it. I'll always count this as a big loss for myself, and for DigitLab. I believed in him and was convinced he could be a big part of our future. Unfortunately, we could not get to that mutual agreement where we both believed in the potential of his future at DigitLab. If someone on your team does not see their potential, you will almost certainly lose him or her, or they will become a liability on your team if they stay.

In the discussions outlined above, I found something important to communicate. You need to clearly communicate the value of this process to the people involved. People may not ask the question: "What's in it for me?" outright, but it is what they're thinking about, most of the time.

If you're looking to unlock the potential within someone, make sure that they're fully committed to the process. Take the time to help them see what's possible and how it will benefit them. When people understand how they will grow and improve, it becomes very exciting to embark on a new journey together.

To close off this chapter, I want to leave you with two practical perspectives on potential:

Firstly, the discussions necessary for unlocking potential can be very inspiring as you look towards the future. They can, however, quickly become challenging as you identify what needs to change in the current day. Change is hard and often painful, and leaders need to recognise that strong emotional intelligence is a big asset in the people you are working with. If people need to develop emotional intelligence before you tackle certain issues, then take the time to develop this – don't rush this process.

Secondly, you can lead a hundred horses to water, but you cannot make them drink. As much as you believe in someone, if they don't believe in themselves, they won't put in the necessary work to unlock their potential. In this situation, I would start these discussions by finding ways to help the person to start believing in him or herself. Find the small wins, celebrate successes and slowly build self-confidence. Once they start believing in themselves and their potential, it will become easier to have the necessary conversations around unlocking it.

7

NARRATIVE OVER VISION

Almost every business leadership book has touted the importance of having a company vision, writing a vision statement, and clearly communicating that vision so that you can lead a group of people in the direction you need.

Vision statements are an important part of leadership. They define your future state and they give the people in your team something to aim for and grow towards. Vision is one of the most important aspects of defining a leadership direction.

As businesses have adopted the process of establishing vision statements, I have unfortunately seen a systematic breakdown of the business value of these statements. Vision statements are becoming far less effective as a means to build team direction, for a number of reasons:

Firstly, a vision statement paints a future picture, which is important, but it doesn't capture the reason you exist. The reason you exist should go beyond what you hope to be in the future and it should govern every decision you make on a daily basis. A future-focused vision can become too detached from the day-to-day world to inspire the kind of actions you are hoping for.

Secondly, there are too many businesses communicating vision statements that all sound the same. Everyone seems to be in pursuit of excellence or looking to add value to their clients' lives. The value of vision statements is being lost in the clutter of jargon and statements that all say the same thing.

Thirdly, a future vision will inspire some people on your team, and others not at all. Every person is different, and inspired by different things. Driven by different dynamics in life, they may or may not be interested in where you are going. Perhaps they are more inspired by how you intend to get there.

I have found that people, especially young people, are more inspired about the place they work for today than what it hopes to be tomorrow. This could be because, as entrepreneurs, we see our business in a long-term view – after all, this business is our personal journey. For employees, however, our company is possibly a small part of their personal journey. Working within our business may not be their ultimate goal. How can a view of the future inspire someone who has a short-term view of his or her role in your business? In today's world, this is becoming more difficult as people tend to be less loyal to a specific company.

That's why I suggest that, in a world of declining company loyalty, we look more towards our own business narrative, rather than focusing on a vision statement. Your business narrative has become far more important to communicate than your vision statement.

Of course, we still need a business vision – we should dream bigger than ever. We should also communicate the vision often and show people our progress towards achieving this vision. It's important and inspiring to be a part of a team that is achieving its goals.

Narrative is, however, different. Narrative brings something new to your culture and your team dynamics. Narrative tells the story of why you exist and everyone loves a good story. Good storytelling draws people in; gives readers or listeners something to connect with; and has an underlying moral that teaches a lesson or challenges a thought. It's difficult to explain my attraction to narrative without sharing my own story with you.

I love being an entrepreneur, but I hated the idea of waking up every morning for the sole purpose of chasing money. At work, I am known as the one chasing the bottom line, making sure we are billing on time and that our sales figures are right. This is my job, and I need to keep an eye on these things to ensure our business is sustainable. It's not, however, what inspires me. I am inspired by and for something completely different. It's taken me a long time to find the words to express this to people.

We did not have a vision statement for DigitLab for the first few years of our operations. We were just trying to do the best possible work for our clients and we loved every minute of it. This approach worked for us because we were a small team, achieving great things through our communal focus. As DigitLab began to grow, it became more difficult to get everyone working the same way and for the same desired output. I started to ask why this was becoming a major challenge as we grew the business. Why were people working differently from the way we had been working for the last few years?

It was only recently that I realised why this was the case. In an interview, Tony Hsieh, CEO of Zappos, was explaining the values at Zappos. Interestingly, he stated that the Zappos values were ultimately his personal values. Watching this interview, I finally realised what was happening in our business. Our fundamental business values weren't working through the business because I was no longer making every decision for and about the business. DigitLab was growing up, and with it, so was our team.

When you are in a small business and you make the majority of the decisions, it's easy to make sure the business works in accordance with your values and towards your goals. You don't need to communicate it through vision statements and narratives because you are making all the decisions. As your business grows, you will empower leaders to make decisions on your behalf and they will do the same. Eventually, you end up with a business whose foundational values are diluted because new leaders bring their own values and aspirations into the picture. It's highly valuable to have diverse leadership styles and passions, but not at the expense of your core values being trampled on.

As we noticed our values becoming diluted, we set out to communicate our vision to the team. We sat down, wrote it out, agreed on values and created a presentation that enabled us to share it with the team. We involved every leader in the communication process, to show the team we all believed in the vision we had set. As we rolled this out, we saw a dramatic change in the business. People could see what we were trying to do and it definitely brought us a little bit closer as a team.

Something was missing though, and it took a lot of time for us to see it. We were driving hard towards our goals but people were slowly becoming a form of collateral damage – an unpleasant side effect of our meeting our goals. I started to hear about people feeling unhappy and some team members even left DigitLab in frustration. As we looked into this, we found that some people loved our vision but set out to achieve it in a way that didn't build people up. Seeing this in action, I began to realise what was important to me – far more important than chasing money. I saw the injustice of people chasing a business vision without taking people into consideration. I realised how, even though I loved helping people win, I had not done the best job at communicating this aspect of my thinking to the team. I wanted to achieve our vision, yes – but I wanted people to love being a part of it, instead of feeling trampled upon to achieve it.

This idea set me on a path to discover our narrative. I finally sat down and wrote our story: the story of why we do what we do, how we do it and what is important to us. I dug the story out for you here:

We are a group of talented people, passionate about digital marketing and business, making the most of our skills in a world that is rapidly changing.

We started out with the simple objective of helping our clients win. They presented a problem to us and we solved it. It was a win-win scenario. One by one, we helped them succeed. Every now and then, we got it wrong but we never stopped trying. These win-win relationships got us recommended for a variety of great business opportunities and, because of this, we are bigger and better today.

We also set out to make sure our employees won as well. We did everything we could to create opportunities for growth, new challenges and mentorship to help people achieve more, every day. We have always been pleasantly surprised by the calibre of people on our team and how they have stepped up to the challenges set before them. We believe that the more we put into the people on our team, the more we are able to deliver better services to our clients and the more likely we will realise our vision.

In the future we hope to be even better at what we do. We firmly believe that we can do this by never letting go of the truth that got us here: always help people win. You will never regret it.

People are the core of our business. Our clients, our shareholders and our employees are people. Helping people win makes them feel happy, proud and appreciated. This is what we want to be known for — making you feel happy, proud and appreciated.

Making sure we are a team who helps people win means that we would be a team that is indispensable to our clients, enjoyable to work with and too painful to lose.

In short, we love helping people win.

It was that last line that helped me discover the very thing that excites me the most about our business. It is what DigitLab was founded upon and it is what was missing in all our communication: We exist to help people win.

It's this business narrative, which I'll unpack in the next chapter, that we hope is the driving force behind what we do. Your business narrative is powerful because it gives you a lens to frame every conversation or engagement you have through the business. Your business narrative is more emotionally driven than a vision. Its independence from the vision means that, even if your vision were to change for some reason, your story would remain the same. Your business narrative reminds you why you exist, and lays out your path towards meeting your business vision.

At DigitLab, whether you are talking to a client, a shareholder or an employee, you should always ask: "How can I help this person win?"

I would encourage every entrepreneur and every business owner to find your narrative as a business. Your company's narrative will help you to scale your leadership and empower your team to know how to act in almost every situation.

To conclude, I want to help you understand the difference between Narrative, Vision, Values and Mission.

- The Narrative: Why we exist
- The Vision: Where we are going
- The Values: How we achieve the vision
- The Mission: What we're currently doing

8

HELPING PEOPLE WIN

Helping people win has become a non-negotiable aspect of business for me. The more I focus on this, the more I find our business meets its targets, more people achieve their dreams and everyone benefits.

Business is about people. It's a simple truth, but one many people lose sight of. Business exists for the benefit of people: shareholders are people; clients and customers are people; employees are people and every aspect of business is people. You will never escape this truth.

The statement "Helping People Win" frames our role as leaders very quickly.

Firstly, we should always focus on people. When a person refers to 'people', they are most likely referring to people other than themselves. The term 'people' points the figure outwards, instead of inwards, and focuses our attention on the right subject. This forces people to be more interested in the problem of the person in front of us, rather than our own problems. We begin to take time to understand people and we learn what it takes to help them succeed. This approach means we will naturally start working with people in a more humble, supportive manner, and one where people will appreciate our work. People always enjoy encounters with us that help them win.

Secondly, helping people win means focusing on the success factors in their world instead of our own. If a sales person is focused on their personal win, they will hound customers to buy and potentially scare people away. Sales people with this approach rarely understand their customers' needs; instead, they push their product onto the client, hoping for the sale. Sales people who take time to understand their clients' environment and success factors will build solid, long-term relationships. Those relationships will enjoy incredible longevity, and their value will far outweigh short-term sales figures.

When we look for the success factors in other people's lives, we start to find the correlations between our goals and theirs. Finding these correlations can be golden opportunities to build strong commitments towards achieving common goals, because they benefit everyone within the relationship.

Finally, when you work to help people win, your relationship and influence with those people always grows stronger. It grows stronger because people can see that you are on their side, that you have their interests at heart and that, ultimately, your success is their success. This is what trust is built on. Never forget that trust is the foundation of influence, and influence is the essence of leadership.

Helping people win should be the narrative for every great leader.

9

CLARITY IS KING

In relationships, life and business, clarity is king. Finding ways to cut through the clutter and noise enables you to find clarity in any and all situations.

When things are clouded, confusion reigns and your ability to chase a vision becomes muddled and eventually lost.

Clarity has been one of our greatest assets and it's something we have spent a lot of time creating and sustaining. Clarity is the simple solution at the end of a complex conversation. Clarity is, after all, a type of knowledge. It is the knowledge of where you stand, what you need to achieve and where you're going.

Clarity is a beautiful gem that sets the playing field for success. It's not how something gets done, it's why we're doing it and knowing what each of us must do. It's the hard work here that has helped us build a stronger business.

I was out on my second date with Stacey when I said something controversial and offered my opinion as though it were the solution to all of life's problems. Stacey replied sharply with: "Well, that's arrogant and unattractive", while she raised her glass of Merlot for another sip. We looked at each other, things turned a little silent and then we burst out laughing. I was hooked.

I will always remember that conversation, because it was a personal pivot point. Stacey took a risk and said something that might have pushed me away or caused a massive argument, but it was worth the risk. She wasn't going to waste her time with just anyone, and she was clear about who she was looking for. She wanted to make sure that we were on the same page, so actively worked to cut right to a clear understanding of who I am.

To be honest, I was spit balling and she knew it. I was trying to look cool and collected, but she was only looking for the real me. I'm glad she was clear about not enjoying the spit balling, because I don't enjoy it either – I was merely nervous about being on the dating scene again, and trying to figure out the right thing to say.

She found the real me, using just a simple, humorous comment. That little piece of clarity showed me that I could be real with her and it set the tone for the rest of our relationship. Today, we're happily married, and we still laugh about it. I'm glad she cut through the noise.

Business is the same. I'll be speaking to a client – we'll call him William for this example. William asks for a proposal on everything we can offer him. I'm happy to do that, but we're meeting for a far more important purpose – so I can better understand his business. That's when I ask him a simple question:

"William, what does success look like for this project?"

William responds: "I want brand awareness."

To which I say: "Great, and how will that be measured at the end of the year by your executive team?"

William replies: "Sales. They want to see a six percent increase in sales of this product by the end of the year."

To be sure, I need to know one more thing: "Does this project need to deliver on that sales target?"

William replies with a "Yes".

The answer to that last question changes everything in our planning. Had I walked away, we would have built a brand awareness project, and at the end of the year his executive would find a lot of brand awareness but not enough sales. This type of situation does not end well for anyone, and normally the agency gets fired.

William has big dreams to unlock the potential within digital services for his business and he's keen to get started. I love clients like William, and that's why I take the time to find the clarity in their needs. I need to find out how to make him look good, how to make real traction in his business and how to deliver a digital service that builds his business, and isn't just talking about it.

I come across many agencies that just take briefs from clients and wonder why the relationship goes sour a few months or years later. Often, it's because you don't understand each other – the agency doesn't understand the client's business and the client doesn't understand the value of the agency. More time should be devoted to building a true business relationship between clients and agencies – understanding each other and being absolutely clear about what you're setting out to achieve.

I meet people like William all the time. Experience has taught me to take the time to find clarity, to get past the jargon and to understand the reasons behind the answers I'm given. It's this hard work, applied throughout our business

FIVE YEAR MARK

relationships, that I believe has been crucial to the success of all of our long-term partnerships.

When DigitLab was launched, there were just two full-time employees, Meegan and I. Paula was working part-time, looking after our accounts, but the rest of the business was up to Meegan and I.

We had to, however, define Meegan's role in the business. Traditionally we'd have needed a job description, but her role was necessarily diverse, enabling us to cater for our clients' needs and our company's growth. After some thought and planning, we found the shortest and best job description and agreement I have ever had at DigitLab:

"I'll (Mike) go out and find new clients and you (Meegan) make sure we don't lose them."

It really was that simple and, within the first year, we had doubled the size of the business. In the second year, it doubled again. That simple piece of clarity meant that we knew we had a lot to do, but we knew what we had to do. We understood what the other person's role was and how to measure them on it. It was a great partnership founded upon a very clear mandate.

A year later, I conducted a project briefing with Natasha, who was new to our team. Meegan was in the room and I was taking Natasha through the project's direction and objectives. I was saying things like: "We want to present to the client on…" and "We need to do research in…" when Meegan interrupted and said to Tash: "Just to be clear, when Mike says 'we', he means you". A little bewildered but determined to do well on this project, Tash agreed and delivered significantly beyond expectation – far more than anything 'we' could have achieved without her.

My favourite quote is a rather famous Leonardo Da Vinci line:

"Simplicity is the ultimate form of sophistication."

It's rich in meaning when you start to apply it. It takes time to find the clarity, so we need to wade through complex conversations, research and scenarios to find the simple truths.

Once you uncover the clarity within a situation or business relationship, these simple outcomes become your most valuable treasures when finding success.

Clarity is King – you will never regret sacrificing your time to this type of royalty.

10

PEOPLE NEED A CHALLENGE

Like most teenagers, I didn't have the greatest self-image. I wasn't the smartest kid on the block. I barely made it through school, believing I was stupid and that I would never really amount to anything. The way I saw it, I wasn't smart, so I may as well enjoy my life. I spent my school days playing water polo, riding bikes, in the gym and organising my social life. After completing my Matric, I spent five months saving money by working as a waiter, and then I set off to travel and work in the United States and the UK. I spent my USA trip on a summer camp where I learnt a lot about running camps for children.

When I returned to South Africa, I spent most of my holidays the next year volunteering at children's camps in the Drakensberg mountains of KwaZulu-Natal. At the end of my first year of volunteering, a respected mentor of mine, Mike Smallbones, challenged me to run the next year's set of camps. I didn't realise it at the time, but this was my first leadership assignment and it propelled me from the schoolboy who thought he was stupid to someone who slowly began to believe in himself.

It was a tough year, because I had to balance my diploma studies with this new role as a camp leader. I was responsible for recruiting a team of volunteers, marketing the camps, designing the camp programme, training the volunteers and so much more.

While the challenge was big, my growth as a person was even bigger. With every decision I made, I grew more confident in myself, and every camp completed was another stream of lessons learnt, memories made and relationships built. This first leadership challenge took me on the biggest growth curve I had ever been on and I loved every minute of it.

T.S. Eliot once said: "If you aren't in over your head, how do you know how tall you are?" It's the challenges that we take on that force us to step up, to become a better version of ourselves, and to realise the potential that lives inside us. If you're not taking on a challenge, chances are you are not planning any growth in your near future. If you're comfortable, then it's highly likely that you're not growing. Within my own life I have learnt that I should be constantly placing myself in challenging positions.

Then I learnt a big leadership lesson. It is the responsibility of the leader to challenge his or her team to bring the best out in them, and to help the team achieve bigger, better, greater things. The leader is not the person who finds the best way to unlock his or her own potential. Instead, a leader must become a professional in unlocking the potential within others. Like Mike Smallbones did with me, I needed to start looking for ways to unlock the potential within others.

This began to be my primary objective in business: to look for potential within people and to find ways to unlock it. I started encouraging people to dream, to find what they loved and to pursue it. I saw my role as someone who builds a business that unlocks the dreams of its employees. At DigitLab, I knew that I'd have to create challenges to enable our team members to do exactly that.

I began launching internal projects, specifically designed to help people see their own potential. I invited people to take part in these projects, over and above their current work. I made sure that everything we did, had as valuable an output as possible and I passed on the credit wherever it was due. The aim was not to do more in DigitLab – it was to help people see their own potential, to throw them into the deep end so that they could see just how tall they really were.

To build a team that can achieve great things, you need to hire talented, skilful and passionate people. There is, however, another important ingredient: you need to challenge these people to become everything they have capacity for. Not every talented individual knows just what he or she may be capable of – it's your responsibility as a leader to find their potential and create a playing field for them to realise it. There's nothing worse than wasted talent.

Since I started leading with this approach, I have seen a number of things happen in the business:

Good people became great people

After presenting challenges to people within our business, we began to see their confidence grow. They began to believe in themselves more and started driving projects within the business on their own. They started setting new challenges, they strived to create better work, they inspired others in the team and they became great assets within our business.

I started losing good people

This isn't exactly the kind of news you want to hear after you've been investing in people and their potential. At first, I was annoyed that this was happening; but I now realise that, if you help people reach their potential, then you need to have somewhere for them to grow to within your business that matches their dream. If you don't, you will lose them and they will pursue more challenging things that unlock their dreams, because you helped them see it was possible. They will chase their dreams and they will hopefully inspire others to do the same.

I am not sad that these people left, because I am happy to see them unlocking their future. I am glad they took a part of their life and used it to help me build DigitLab, and I wish them well as they take on their next challenge.

Passion became real and tangible

The people who work at DigitLab are people who are passionate about the DigitLab business and vision. They love the work we do and feel that their work matters, as we chase down our common dream.

Each challenge we present to people is an opportunity for people to grow. They grow by spending their most precious resource, time, by pouring their energy and talents into DigitLab. They see the success and feel the value they bring to the table, which then produces passion at an exponential rate.

Passion is powerful and it has come to life because everyone within our team is encouraged to take up the challenges we set and to help us get to the next step. We all contribute to getting us there and we all share the credit and reward once we do. It's hard not to be passionate when you know you helped build a business you believe in.

We do more

Business is all about input and output. The more challenges we create within our business, the more we are encouraging people to input – and their input naturally creates higher levels of output. The added bonus is that people are proud of the output they produce. This sense of achievement and pride is addictive and we see more and more people within our business driving for more challenging scenarios and projects. As a result, we produce a higher quality output as a business.

The more we output, the more the industry sees us; and the more we work with different clientele, the higher our quality of work goes. In a sense, our drive to challenge people to their full potential is our best marketing vehicle because it produces our best work, which then speaks for itself. Our reputation as an agency that excels has, through this approach, been built on our ability to attract incredible talent, and then to give them a big enough challenge.

11

WHY WE DON'T DELEGATE

A leader always needs people around him or her who can help make things happen. Often, many leaders do not lean on the excellent people around them, and end up spending more of their time in the business, rather than on the business.

This is a common business problem which often leads people to become ineffective leaders.

Over the past five years, I have found three reasons why leaders often don't delegate work to their employees or peers:

We don't trust others to do it

It is that simple: we are surrounded by people we do not trust to do a good job. Entrepreneurs often don't spend enough time with their team to build up their skills in doing the work the right way.

Solution: Hire well and train better.

Hire and partner with trustworthy people. Then, spend a lot of time at the beginning of your journey with them, ensuring that they know and understand how to do what you need them to do.

Self-importance

This often happens when we get into a rut on the first problem. When we are constantly let down by untrustworthy employees or employees who weren't trained properly, we begin to believe a massive lie:

"Only I can do this correctly. I just have to find the time to do it."

This attitude is a recipe for disaster and often ends up in broken businesses, broken lives and possibly a few hospital visits.

Solution: Humility.

You can coach and lead others to do the same things you do. They may even be better suited to do the job than you.

Guilt

I shouldn't make my problems anyone else's problem. They didn't sign up for this. I should bear the brunt of the challenge and let them handle the easy stuff.

Solution: Consider a new perspective.

When you give people on your team new challenges, they have the opportunity to prove themselves and grow within your business. The harder the challenge, the bigger their opportunity for growth will be.

Warning: When people grow, you by default will have to grow. New roles will have to be created, because the people in your team are driving your business forward. The delegation of ownership over business problems allows your business and your team to grow faster within your business.

You will need to grow in your leadership abilities, so that you are able to keep up with those people on your team who are stepping up to the challenges you present them.

People want to grow, and growth is possible through delegation. Keep in mind that people might actually want you to delegate.

FIVE YEAR MARK

THE NUTS AND BOLTS OF OUR BUSINESS

"Good is the enemy of great, that's why so few things become great"
Jim Collins

MIKE SAUNDERS

12

MASTERS OF INDUSTRY

One of my very best life experiences took place during a meeting with a prospective client. They'd asked us if we had built a particular mobile application, and I proudly responded in the affirmative, eagerly waiting for their response.

I was blown away as they relayed back to me that their entire business unit, which was building its own application, was using our application as the standard to beat. They recognised our application as being the best of its class within their industry.

Another of my favourite moments happened as I was reading a local research report, where our client was noted as being one of the most responsive brands in South Africa. It was great to know that our team was actively behind every single online response that the brand made.

The day I found out that we had helped a client go from 30 to 300 leads a month was another great day. To top it off, the leads were strong enough to attract a 90 percent close rate from their sales team.

In 2014, I bumped into a well-respected industry thought leader while on business in Mauritius. I was so encouraged to hear that he had enjoyed our white paper on using LinkedIn, and he thanked us for releasing it.

Delivering excellent work is not the easiest thing to do, but it is highly rewarding. This is why so many businesses include the word 'excellence' in their vision statements, objectives or company goals. Of course, that has led to the word losing some meaning, especially because every customer rightly demands a level of delivery excellence from the businesses they support.

Delivering excellent work or products to customers is no longer a competitive advantage. You are not better because you provide excellence to your customer; excellence is expected. The level of excellence in most industries is already so high that aiming for excellence is no longer a viable competitive edge. It's simply the standard foundation for any good business. It's not a negotiable extra, it's not added value and it's definitely not what differentiates you.

FIVE YEAR MARK

If you are hoping that delivering excellent work will set you apart, you're wrong. Nowadays, delivering excellence simply means that you will meet the expectations of your customer.

I recently watched a TED video where Sarah Lewis shared a story of archers aiming at a target. She watched as each archer drew back the bow, took aim and hit the target. They would spend hours dedicated to repeating this practice over and over again. Hitting the target once was important, but it meant absolutely nothing unless they could do it over and over again.

According to Sarah, if excellence is hitting the target, then mastery is the ability to hit it over and over again.

Excellence is fleeting but mastery adds real value.

This thought changed my idea of chasing excellence. It set the goal higher: we had to become masters of our industry. Masters of a craft make the craft look easy. They work through their craft quickly, while taking others under their wing to teach them. Masters have moved beyond excellence and stepped towards becoming significant. They actively contribute to their craft or industry, instead of simply wielding it.

When I was learning to play the drums, I was taught to play each note on the beat. It's important for drummers never to miss the beat, to be steady in the timing and not speed up or slow down. Learning to play on the beat is an important part of drumming, but great drummers find a way to move beyond the timing.

If the beat is 1, 2, 3, 4 then playing on the beat will mean you're perfectly on time. You're not wrong, but there is something clinical about the sound you create. It seems too perfect, too rigid and lacks groove.

Being able to create a groove entails knowing how to bend the beat to your will. Leaving the right gaps in the music, playing ahead of the beat to give a rushed feel or hanging back to create space, making the music feel slower without actually slowing down.

Good drummers play on time, while master drummers use the timing as a guide and bend the beat to their will, creating groove that you can't stop moving to.

In business, we mustn't simply stop at excellence. We should work to become masters, and our work should become something inspirational to behold. It's through committing ourselves to mastery, that we inspire others to do better and produce even better work.

FIVE YEAR MARK

Talented people are attracted towards industry masters. While you may be pursuing mastery for the sake of your clients or business, talented people are attracted towards you, because they want to work with the best, so that they are able to be a part of the best work.

In the advertising world, there are many awards programmes that agencies can participate in, competing for coveted awards that prove they are masters of their industry. Nearly every award-winning agency will tell you that winning awards does more for attracting great talent than it does for generating new business. Great talent follows the industry masters, just as the apprentice works for the best craftsman he or she can find.

Choosing to become a master of your industry will help you to deliver consistent excellence to your customer, but also enable you to attract the best talent to your team.

13

(1 + 1) > 2

I have never been a genius with Mathematics – far from it, in fact. My dad was an accountant and all those mathematical skills appear to have been passed on to my brother who is now an engineer in Canada. I am more of a strategic thinker, someone who looks at possibility and doesn't get weighed down by the numbers. I am forever optimistic that we can somehow make the numbers work.

Perhaps then only people who think like I do would find peace with writing an equation of [(1+1) > 2]. I can see my brother's eye already twitching as I try to validate my completely illogical mathematical equation.

My attempt at a mathematical truth does, however, make complete sense when I apply it to the concept of partnerships. Good partnerships should be exponential and not additional. I'll explain by sharing some experiences with you.

FIVE YEAR MARK

A year after starting Mike Saunders Consulting – a very badly named consulting firm that was my stopgap between employment and starting DigitLab – a local advertising agency approached me to start a digital agency with them. They wanted me to head it up, take all my learning and thinking and apply it to their client base, both current and future. It sounded terribly exciting.

DigitLab had not even started yet, and I was working as a consultant out of my home office. The conversations that followed were a thrill as we talked through the possibilities attached to joining forces.

After a few meetings, we began to talk about the financial terms, shareholding structures and workload. I started to see that the agency was willing to back the business financially, but didn't have a resource infrastructure that was cost-effective enough for me to work with. If I were to partner with this agency, I couldn't provide the services I was providing to my existing clients at the rates I had agreed to. I had committed to specific outcomes for my clients and I wanted to see them through.

The other issue lay in that I would be the only person building the business. The partnership opportunity on the table didn't add to my digital resources or my ability to build a digital agency. Although they were happy to provide the financial backing to create this new division, I didn't feel there was a shared ownership in our success. If they planned to build this digital division only to serve their current client base, it would be suitable for their needs, but not for mine. I was eager to grow, create and build a company, not just to add on to someone else's.

That's why, on a warm November day in 2009, I inhaled deeply and presented them with the cheekiest business partnership proposal, I think, ever written. It was so cheeky that it may have even come across as offensive or arrogant. I was intentional in this, hoping they'd turn me down. It was a sales pitch on why you shouldn't invest in me right now. I was trying to show them that a partnership between the two of us was not an exponential partnership and that we would be no better off in a partnership, than out of partnership. They agreed and we called it quits.

The experience did, however, offer some truly great outcomes. I was able to keep my current clients, most of whom are still with DigitLab today.

I met Meegan, who later became DigitLab's first full-time employee. I started to believe in the DigitLab dream and began planning the launch of my favourite business venture to date. As it turned out too, I'd saved enough capital to start DigitLab on my own, so I no longer needed the financial backing that agency could have offered me.

Partnerships should make you better, not bigger. One plus one should equal far more than just two. Together, you should be able to do infinitely more than you can do apart, otherwise there's really no point. You'd simply add your businesses together, turn the same profit margin and become a slightly bigger version of yourself. Within that process though, you'd inherit each other's business problems and, as you grow, those problems multiply.

I do have a far more positive partnership story that centres on how Steve Gardner joined our DigitLab team as both a shareholder and Chief Technical Officer (CTO).

Steve and I have a longstanding friendship, and he's one of the smartest people I know in the digital space.

We first crossed paths in the Durban music scene – he was a trumpeter in a ska-punk band that was super famous around Durban and I was a teenager, dreaming of becoming a rock star, doing everything possible to get into his concerts.

Steve had been running a web development company for twelve years before he joined DigitLab. During that time, he began to notice a shift in the digital arena, as businesses needed more specialised marketing skills to succeed online. He was concerned that his boutique web development company might lose relevance if it didn't offer marketing services. Meanwhile, I was in the DigitLab office a few kilometres up the road from him, realising that we would lose our market relevance if we didn't start building a mobile development resource.

An unexpected email arrived in my inbox. It was Steve, asking if he could use my blog as a base to build a mobile application for a competition he was entering. It was one of the many fun side projects he was involved in, and he is the type of person who always invests in a cool hobby. (As I write this, he's working on building a small brewery in his garage.)

That application turned into a life-changing conversation that ultimately started one of the most powerful partnerships I have ever entered into.

We agreed entirely that our businesses needed each other, so that we could not only remain relevant but also grow in the ways we wanted them to.

We both knew we would have to invest in each other to make this work, and we knew that there was far more to this partnership than simply merging two businesses. We knew this partnership would be exponential.

Since then Steve and I have built a mobile business at DigitLab that has become a core part of our value offering to customers. We have been able to help brands corner new markets with mobile apps; built websites for companies all over the world; and we have helped to launch start-up businesses. Most recently, we designed and built a new product for the digital marketing industry called Monocle, which provides real-time social intelligence for our clients.

The last few years of our partnership have proven the exponential power within it. As we have grown and nurtured DigitLab, it's been difficult yet fun. We've both felt like giving up at times, but our growth and ability to overcome obstacles has always been stronger because we are more than just $1 + 1$.

That's why my seemingly illogical mathematical equation makes sense. Partnerships should be about building a robust team of people who, together, are far more powerful than they are on their own.

14

CHART YOUR OWN COURSE

My lovely wife left me with no option one evening but to watch "Runaway Bride". I'm more of a "Lord of The Rings" fan, and Julia Roberts' pursuits in a wedding gown and sneakers don't really interest me.

"Runaway Bride" is, essentially, a movie about understanding yourself before you can find love. In the movie, Maggie Carpenter, played by Julia Roberts, has no idea who she really is. She restructures her life, habits and dreams around the person she's currently dating. The most notable way she does this is to have her eggs cooked exactly the way her fiancé likes his eggs. She ends up running away from not just one, but three, fiancés on three separate wedding days. Throughout the movie, she battles to understand why she does this.

In the end, she spends time deconstructing her life and finding out who she really is. She sets out to sell her lighting designs in New York, finally settles on her favourite way to cook eggs, and the movie ends with her proposing to her love interest, Ike Graham, played by Richard Gere.

In the proposal scene she explains why she runs on her wedding day:

> *Maggie Carpenter: I wanted to tell you why I run – sometimes ride – away from things.*
> *Ike Graham: Does it matter?*
>
> *Maggie Carpenter: I think so.*
>
> *[takes a deep breath]*
>
> *Maggie Carpenter: When I was walking down the aisle I was walking towards somebody who didn't have any idea who I really was. And it was only half the other person's fault, because I had done everything to convince him that I was exactly what he wanted. So it was good that I didn't go through with it because it would have been a lie. But you – you knew the real me.*
>
> *Ike Graham: Yes, I did.*
> *Maggie Carpenter: I didn't. And you being the one at the end of the aisle didn't just fix that.* (IMDb, 2016)

Maggie then goes on to explain that it wasn't enough that Ike knew who she was – she needed to know for herself.

In marriage, in life and in business, it's great when someone believes in you, but you need to start believing in yourself. You need to develop a certain level of self-awareness and understand the motive behind your decisions.

I have met many business people who run their business in a particular way because that's the way their business partner does, or that's how it's always been done, or it's what they call 'best practice'. While there's nothing inherently wrong with this approach, we need to dig deeper to find out why we do things the way we do. If you want to apply a process, a rule, a practice or even a value to your business, you should understand why it's there and challenge it until it makes sense to you.

Thereafter, you should only apply it to your business if you absolutely believe that it is the best option for you and your business. Don't simply do something because it worked for someone else and, even worse, don't apply a 'best practice' technique just because it exists.

A few years ago a friend, Theran Knighton-Fitt, wrote a book called "Re:thingk". In this philosophical book about belief in God, Theran set out to challenge people on their thinking. He wanted them to investigate and discover why they believed exactly what they believed. Theran wasn't trying to disprove a belief system. Instead, he wrote "Re:thingk" to encourage people to actively invest in their belief systems and empower them to understand their reasons for believing. He encouraged people to deconstruct their belief and reconstruct it again, hoping that the reconstructive process would make their belief stronger and more real than ever before.

I have always liked that approach from Theran – it made him a great teacher and a brilliant creative individual. I also agree wholeheartedly with him, because I meet many people who don't truly understand why they do what they do.

In starting DigitLab, I bucked against the trend often. I often chose not to adopt any 'best practice' technique until we truly understood why we should. I prioritised our cash flow because I understood the value of cash, and it enabled us to breathe as a business. I chose a flexi-time approach to our workdays, because I believed I needed to respect the time of our employees. I chose a profit-sharing bonus model because I believed it would be the best for the business and the employees.

When we decided to conduct annual performance reviews, we did so because it was a business 'best practice' and some people had asked for it. As a system, it failed miserably for us, because it didn't solve the problems our employees were having quickly enough – and it made our human resources processes cumbersome and ineffective. Once we stopped running annual performance reviews, we designed a mentoring programme that keeps every member of our team accountable, on a bi-weekly and monthly basis.

Similarly, we explored a 'best practice' sales process, which resulted in our losing a large amount of capital, because we could not transfer valuable knowledge to our sales people quickly enough. Our sales approach is completely different now and has been designed around our unique set of capabilities and resources.

Just as Theran challenged his readers to know why they believe, and just as Maggie needed to spend time discovering her own motivations, I challenge business people to know why they do what they do.

Deconstructing the processes of your business, and the 'best practice' techniques you're told to use, enables you to ensure that you can achieve what you set out to.

Don't be shaped by the processes of your competitors and peers. Your situation, size, circumstances, resources and abilities are most likely different from anyone else's. Shape your solutions around your needs and work to solve the unique business problems your company has. Chart your own course and do what is right for your business.

Many agencies within our related industries use the same project management system. When our MD, Darren Young, began to explore project management systems, he decided not to use the industry choice. Instead, he opted for one a client had used for a particular project. He chose it because of its agility, simplicity and cost-effectiveness. The industry standard system had been developed around advertising processes, most of which were designed by bigger agencies that need robust, safe and secure processes. Our business is smaller and one of our key operational goals is agility.

We must be able to move quickly when the opportunities present themselves. The system Darren chose allowed us to do that, and it still does. We bucked the trend to be more like the business we wanted to be instead of the business the industry expects us to be.

Another industry 'best practice' lies in the concept of awards. Many agencies chase awards, sometimes even selling a client a service or product that is deliberately award-winning, instead of doing what the client actually needs. The awards industry always seems filled with contradiction and controversy and, as a result, I was reluctant to get involved.

Nevertheless, we began entering our work into award-focused competitions, because we believed it was a great marketing exercise, and of course it was considered 'best practice'. I remained uncomfortable with this notion until I had a brief conversation with the Loeries CEO, Andrew Human, who cleared up the awards process for me.

Awards ceremonies do not exist as a marketing tool, nor are they magical techniques for attracting great talent – those are the side effects of winning awards. Awards exist to create a yardstick against which you can measure your creativity.

You may not like the yardstick, but it works as a tool to sift out the best work from the industry. Awards exist to improve the level of excellence and creativity in your business and industry. Awards like the Loeries are an industry-recognised process that seeks to inspire and encourage higher levels of excellence in advertising agencies.

Now that I was able to deconstruct the awards business, I understood it for its purpose. Nowadays, we have a specific business strategy that focuses on winning awards, but not for marketing or ego-related purposes. Our desire to win awards is rooted in our desire to be better, more creative, and more innovative. It's tough, but important, to reach our full potential as an agency.

Through deconstructing why you do things the way you do, you may find that the best practices actually work for you, just as the awards industry works for us.

FIVE YEAR MARK

15

CASH HELPS YOU BREATHE

If you have read Chapter 13, then you will know that – in the midst of negotiating a business partnership to start DigitLab – I looked back into my bank account and realised I had enough money to start the business on my own.

It was a relief to find that I had the resources to launch the business I wanted to. It helped me think clearly and focus more on what type of company I wanted to build, instead of how much money I needed to run it. It gave me a little space to breathe, enabling me to focus on the business' possibilities, rather than the initial tight cash flow problem every new business owner faces.

I wish I could tell you that having cash in my account as I reached an important partnership discussion was planned. It wasn't. I had simply put my head down from day one of consulting, only paid myself what I needed to live, and left the rest in the bank. I never really looked at how much cash was in the account for the first ten months of working for myself. I was driven by a fear of not being able to support my family and that's all there was to it. There was no clever strategy or complicated spreadsheet – I was purely determined to work as hard as possible to look after my family.

In hindsight, I realise that what I was doing, was building breathing room into my life. Quietly building that cash base enabled me to dissolve my fears and focus on the business I wanted to create. To do this, I adopted a very simple philosophy:

Cash first, then work

I structured my billing process to ensure that I earned set-up fees, research fees, training fees and deposit payments for projects. I also began charging for proposals, because I knew – all too well – of the trap that many young entrepreneurs fall into. You know the one: you end up doing work for free because it's good for your portfolio, or undercharging for your services because you're worried your rates will scare off a client. I decided to start billing quickly and early in client relationships so that I could not only test the waters, but set a precedent.

I began to understand that when I pitch for new work, the client is not only interviewing me, but I should also be interviewing the client. I'd ask these questions (mostly to myself) and then assess the suitability of a potential client relationship:

- Can they afford the value of my services?
- Will the client see my services as valuable?
- Does the client have a solid business model that needs my agency?
- Do I trust and believe in their product or service?

I found polite ways to turn down work and discovered that, by charging upfront, I was able to work with a select group of great clients who not only usually paid on time, but also believed in our business and trusted us to do our job to the best of our ability.

The next three years of DigitLab were incredible. We couldn't stop growing, there was cash in the account and everyone was happy. We were able to spend money on developing a great culture and pay bonuses to our staff at the end of each year.

Then year four arrived: 2014. We made two big decisions that year. The first was to grow our client base, which saw us initiating a large new business strategy. This new strategy led to our spending half our capital within a year, without generating much new business. It was an expensive error, but I'm glad we made it. We learnt a lot, and we tried something new. The day we stop trying will be the day I accept defeat and close up shop.

The second decision was just as big, and it required an investment that took up the other half of our cash reserves. The idea behind it was initiated during a conversation with Steve Gardner, our CTO. We were discussing where the next innovative step needed to be taken within DigitLab.

Steve was convinced that data was our next step. This excited me, because I have always felt that the value in social media does not lie in the platforms, but rather in the opportunities the platforms offer to better understand customers.

We chatted about the need for marketers to be more agile in marketing and how there were limited tools out there to help them understand social data in a few seconds. If they could do that, they could make the right decisions quickly. We grew very excited about the idea of real-time social data and how it could change the way marketers were implementing social media marketing.

We commissioned part of our development team to begin a few months of investigation and exploration. On a Monday evening early in December, we called various players on our team together to discuss and plan our first product. There was an awesome atmosphere in the room as our development team highlighted the possibilities and as Steve and I shared what we were hoping to achieve. As a team, we devoured pizza, drew mind-maps, put together sketches and product options. At the end of the evening, we decided to build Monocle, and launch it in March 2015. It would be a mammoth task, but every person on our team believed in it, and committed to creating it.

For me, the decision was tougher than previous business ventures we had embarked upon at DigitLab. In the past, we had started new divisions by building the intellectual property and selling the service as we developed the resources. Service-focused businesses are great like that – you scale your resources in line with the demand.

Monocle was a different beast though, because it demanded up-front resourcing and investment, before we could show it to a client. My 'cash first, then work' philosophy wasn't going to work here. I was excited and nervous, so I used every available minute I had thinking about how we were going to make this happen.

I knew that by pursuing Monocle, we would lose our breathing room and that things were going to get tough. Committing our cash reserves to a project would mean that intense pressure would be placed on other areas of our business, to keep it in good shape.

We kept an even closer eye on our accounts, to ensure we could pay the bills and manage our cash flow effectively. We had to halt the wonderful but expensive culture projects that supported our team. This caused some frustration within our team as we came across as not caring about the people within our company.

This, of course, wasn't true. We cared deeply about our people and did everything we could to explain that this was temporary. Highlighting that we needed to invest in Monocle and recover from some losses helped, and I took on a mentorship role with our middle management team too. Through this, I encouraged them as they found ways to grow and support their teams within a limited framework. Whatever we lacked through not spending money, we made up for by investing time and energy into our people.

Unfortunately we did lose some people along the way, but the team that stayed through 2014 has become incredibly valuable to us. Their commitment shone during this time, and we saw people improve their quality of work, step into leadership roles, commit to bigger outcomes and deliver on them. It's incredible to be part of a team that remains committed to our cause, even when resources are low. In a strange way, our lack of breathing room helped show us those who were truly dedicated to the team.

Initially, having cash in the bank gave us some breathing room. This helped us start the business, make better strategic decisions, build products and try new business ventures. We used the space to dream about the future of the industry and our business.

FIVE YEAR MARK

When we began using our breathing room to grow, as highlighted in Chapter 10, we started to see more from our people.

Ultimately, cash helps you to breathe deeply, to take a long term view, to make good choices and to resource growth properly.

The simplest way to obtain this breathing room is to keep a careful eye on your business profit lines. If you are consistently profitable, then you can and will build more breathing room.

We have also found that breaking down our profit lines to divisions and cost centres helped us to understand the way the business was working. We could see which division was performing well, which was under-resourced and where we were most profitable. This separation of profit lines became a useful decision-making tool for our team, enabling us to improve our profits and create more breathing room in our own business.

These are my three tips for building breathing room in your business:

- Develop a reporting process that tracks every aspect of your business and helps you understand how your profit line is doing;

- Keep on top of your debtors and creditors lists; and
- Build a detailed budget that outlines the costs attached to achieving your goals. Then add your profit line and gear your business towards hitting that target.

A quick side note on Monocle

Although we used our breathing room to grow and innovate, there is one thing I would now do differently in both these cases: identify markers against which to measure progress.

These markers would tell me, very quickly, whether or not something was working. Sometimes you will need to pull the plug on a venture – and it's good to know it sooner rather than later.

Two years after launching Monocle, we made the decision to shut it down. We had built a great product and people were buying it. Unfortunately, we were unable to get a sales process running fast enough to fund the innovation cycle. It was simply too expensive to run with a small sales volume.

If we had put markers in place, we would have realised, early on, that we would need to approach investors with this idea to see it succeed. Monocle was a big idea that needed a faster development timeline and a bigger sales pipeline than we had access to. We needed help to make it happen, but we took too long to work it out.

Innovation is an important part of our business and we will always look to improve. The biggest lesson I gained through our Monocle experience lay in learning when to shut a project down, and when to bring the partners in. If you don't, you run the risk of draining your company's profitability, resources and potential.

16

FOCUS ON OUTPUT

During a meeting in Johannesburg, a client told me of his frustrations with service providers. Essentially, he felt frustrated because he had so many people around him with great ideas, yet nobody seemed equipped to execute them well.

I left that meeting reminded that, unless your service business can deliver on its promises in a clean and efficient manner, then you might as well stop what you're doing.

The idea is important but the execution is what customers actually need. They need people who can get things done.

I've had many more conversations like this, including discussions with young entrepreneurs looking for investment. They have a great idea and an interested investor but, before committing, the investor wants to see something built, tangible or operational.

Investors are even happy to see an entrepreneur failing, because they can see they are learning. A stagnant, frozen entrepreneur who is still trying to get buy-in to an idea or who is waiting for the right conditions, proves absolutely nothing to potential investors and customers. Getting up, making things happen and producing some work is the way forward. Creating a catalogue of output and a portfolio of work is as important as finding someone to invest in you.

Over the last five years, we have placed a considerable focus on being able to get things done – ensuring that we were always creating something that got released, produced and launched. As a young business, we had to prove that we could not only get the job done, but that we would get it done well.

There is a big problem being the new kid on the block. People may see you as innovative, smart and sexy, but they unconsciously also feel that you are young and ignorant of the challenges of business. As a young business, you have to do your level best to ensure your clients can take you seriously, by delivering on your promises and getting things done.

We took this idea of creating output in the business to the extreme in some cases, not only by delivering on promises to customers, but also by building our own passion projects.

Delivering on promises

Within our first year, we set out to deliver on our promises to customers. After our first year of business, we had a number of case studies we could speak about and use as a marketing tool, to encourage others to work with us.

Creating our own passion projects

We created and implemented our own passion projects. During our first years, DigitLab became renowned for creating useful resources for our industry. We wrote manuals on how to use social networks, released informative infographics and produced research reports on a variety of topics. Our focus on internal passion projects has enabled us to continue creating things we care about, and that serve our industry – including Monocle, DigitLab Insights, The DigitLab Academy, Digital Swarm and this book.

Our keen focus on output helped us to build a reputation as a business that can, and will, deliver on its promises. Over time, we realised that the industry saw us punching above our weight, doing things you'd only expect from bigger agencies. We might be a small team, but we can help clients achieve big things.

FIVE YEAR MARK

Produce work that counts, consistently. Become professional about not only creating great work, but about finishing and releasing it too. Always focus on your output, not just your input.

17

NEVER PITCH OVER THE PHONE

Just yesterday, I was out on a ride with a friend, a fellow entrepreneur. As we chatted, he began to share his experiences with cold calling. He's just launched his business and feels ready to start selling, but the responses he's receiving are lukewarm and mostly negative. He asked me how we handle cold calling, and I had to admit that we struggle with this aspect of our business too.

I hate cold calling. I think most people do, but it is only one of the many ways we can use to increase the exposure of our business in a personal manner. Calling people up and talking about our company should surely turn into business at some point. Surely?

Unfortunately, in my experience, this never works. Cold calling presumes that we need to tell the person on the other end of the telephone everything about our company and what it can do for them, in the hope that it'll entice the person to buy from us. In the process, it leaves little to no room for you to learn about their business.

That said, cold calling can be a useful tool in discovering potential new clients or partners, and weeding out the ones you don't need. In this sense, cold calling techniques are an important skill to learn because, in some way, you will never stop using them. Every entrepreneur will spend a big part of his or her life in a cold calling environment. You may not be directly selling your product or service, but you may need to use cold calling to reach out to potential clients, prospective talent or investors. It's important to understand how cold calling works, and how to make the most out of it.

Here are my essential guidelines for cold calling:

Beware the time waster

If you are not speaking to the decision maker, or the person who can get you access to the decision maker, then you're wasting your time.

There are so many time wasters who have invited me for meetings, chatted to me about how great our business is and how they desperately they need our services. These people seem passionate and excited about us, but don't have the resources or decision-making power to start a business relationship. Do your best to ensure that you're speaking to the right people. If you do decline the requests of a time-waster, do it politely and kindly. There's a good chance that today's time-waster will be tomorrow's decision-maker. No matter what, always treat people with respect, honour your commitments and act professionally.

Help people win

Our narrative at DigitLab is "Helping People Win". This ethos is embedded into everything we do, so it makes sense that I would look to embed this into our sales cycle. If I approach a sales call I now look for the win: *their win*. The person on the other side of the call needs to win and I need to find out how to make that happen. To do that, I have learnt to flip the conversation from a series of 30-second elevator pitches to a set of questions that strike at the heart of the problem I know I can solve for them.

Switch to questions that find out what they do, what they need to achieve, what they need to achieve their results, how results are measured and what they see as success. Focusing on their business is key, in the same way a doctor focuses on your symptoms instead of on her qualifications.

No one likes a know-it-all, and people prefer to know you have their interests at heart. In your first encounter, you should do everything you can to help them know that. You need to make it clear that you are here to help them win.

Curiosity and relevance

I found this bit of brilliance in a conversation with a friend and fellow digital enthusiast, Neil Vose. I asked him what he felt opened the most doors for him. His answer was, simply: "curiosity and relevance". I appreciate the simplicity of this approach and the way it again focuses the 'seller' on the person they are speaking to. How can I spark curiosity in the person on the other side, and how can I prove to them that I'm relevant?

When I speak to someone I wish to sell a service to, I want to leave them with a sense of curiosity. Curiosity lingers in their mind, which then makes what I've said over the telephone something for them to think about. Curiosity keeps me front-of-mind for them and helps me step out of their logical thought processes, moving instead to the emotional ones. Nearly every human decision is made with an emphasis on emotions, so I need to ensure I can get my potential client's emotional buy-in.

Relevance is the catalyst in the conversation. If what I am saying is relevant to your current circumstances, you are more likely to commit to further conversations. If I am not relevant to your world, but have sparked your curiosity, I am nothing but a welcome distraction.

Coupling curiosity and relevance will help you design your pitch conversation to land the next meeting.

Sell a meeting, not a product

This simple revelation changed the idea of cold calling for me. It's all about the meeting, not the service or product. I went from selling the product to trying to get the meeting. I would try to understand your wins, present myself in a relevant manner that made you curious, and then ask for a meeting.

In a cold call, I do not discuss the product anymore because that's what the meeting is for. I won't send an email, because I want the meeting, and I won't settle for anything less than the meeting. If you choose not to meet with me, then I didn't understand your needs; I was not relevant to you or you weren't curious enough.

In short, when cold calling:

- Focus on finding out what their win is;
- Position yourself as the solution in a way that builds curiosity and proves relevance; and
- Sell the meeting, not the product.
- Now that you have a meeting, you have the right platform to pitch your solution. Enjoy it, and make it count.

18

PLAY THE END GAME

The main driver of our company's success has been our strong, long-term relationships with partners and clients. We would not have reached our five year mark without them, and without our mutual commitment to creating and sustaining these long-term relationships.

The fact that some of our clients have been with us for over five years is one of the aspects of our business that I am most proud of – especially considering that the industry average is a three-year relationship between a client and agency.

One of our very first clients was one of the bravest people I have ever met. She asked us for help with implementing social media platforms, strategy and marketing for her business, and convinced her board to redirect their marketing budget towards a website and social media presence. Her board members were not supportive of the idea, but let her run with it for a short trial period.

The pressure was on – we had six months to prove to her board that social media would realise returns for her business. We launched a website and a few social channels, while implementing a carefully crafted strategy. The results were astounding, directly impacting our client's sales margin and making a huge difference to their business. It was such a triumph for my client and I was proud to be a part of it.

We managed that client's social media needs for a few years after that, until they took the decision to move it in-house. I was initially nervous and concerned that we were losing a client. I decided to play the long game, and instead of focusing on losing a client, chose to build a long-lasting relationship. I began to grow excited about the transition they were making and we decided to support them in any way possible. We did everything we could to support them and helped to train their team, ensuring that they could operate independently of us.

A little while later, this client approached us to build a mobile application for their business, and they needed some strategic direction. Today, we are still partnering with them as we execute their mobile strategy.

Sometimes, the nature of a relationship may change but that does not mean the relationship needs to end. This particular client has been with us for a long time, and we are still working together, five years later.

The two biggest lessons we've learnt about building these relationships are:

It takes time

Anyone who knows me well knows that I am not a patient person. In relationship building, I have had to learn the art of letting time unfold. It hasn't come easily to me, but it's always been worth it.

You cannot expect to build high volumes of trust within just a few months – it takes time and shared experiences to build a relationship. To ensure we build trust and rapport, we focus on the following principles:

- Communicate often;
- Deliver on promises;
- Say sorry when you mess up; and
- Help them achieve their goals.

It doesn't mean sacrificing now for later

This happens in almost every industry – all too often,

potential new clients ask for a service or product to be delivered at a lower rate, or within a shorter time frame than you can deliver. Eager to scoop a new client, many companies or entrepreneurs fall into this trap. We're swayed by the promises of future work and the idea of building a long-term relationship and we don't realise we are sacrificing our own needs. In doing whatever it takes to impress the new client, we forget that:

Someone always pays the balance

It's either a staff member working overtime unnecessarily, another client being pushed out for the new deal, or the work you deliver to the new client not being at your usual quality standard. In every case, someone chips in the extra to make up for the fact that you undervalued the promise you were making to the client.

We work to create impressive products, to deliver on time and enable ourselves to feel good about doing this for our clients. But we also need to consider the pain it will bring to our business – someone always pays the balance.

You set the tone for the future

If you start a relationship by sacrificing something, you will always be expected to make the sacrifice. The exception you made on the first delivery will become the norm, and

FIVE YEAR MARK

you will constantly be in a sacrifice mode with this new relationship. It won't be long before you realise that this relationship is not working, and you need to find a way out. These situations can, however, be overcome through having a robust and honest conversation. In most cases, you should be able to turn it around – but try not to start with a sacrifice.

19

WORK ON THE BUSINESS

Entrepreneurs are often dubbed workaholics because of how hard we work. We tend to have more on our plate than we can handle, and some entrepreneurs really struggle to prioritise the right things.

In the early days of starting DigitLab, I tried to do everything, diligently staying up every night, waking up early and spending as much time as possible getting through my to-do list. It took about a year to realise that this wasn't working. It wasn't sustainable, smart or helping my clients (or me).

I still believe entrepreneurs should work hard, but only on the things that matter. We should not be caught up in 'busyness', but rather focus on our business.

Our attention should be caught by our dreams, aspirations and vision, not someone else's. If we don't take control of our time, someone else will – possibly an investor, a customer or even a well-meaning employee. An unfocused entrepreneur is dangerous for their business. They can become demotivated and dysfunctional, losing their vision and feeling of achievement as they chase it down.

I know this to be true, because I experienced the same thing in year four of DigitLab. I had spent my last year doing the day-to-day agency work that I loved, but I was not inspired, excited and enjoying my work. I realised it was because I had lost the momentum of working towards our vision. My days were being spent managing the business, instead of working on building the business. Realising this was a major breakthrough towards restructuring our business, helping us to build again and renew our passion for the vision we had.

Productivity, for an entrepreneur, is not about doing things faster. It's about being able to cut through the clutter to find the right things to focus your time on. Productivity, for the entrepreneur, is about finding clarity and purpose in your day, instead of checking off a to-do list.

In my time as an entrepreneur, I have found the following tips very helpful in becoming a more valuable asset to my business:

Set daily goals and achieve them

Entrepreneurs are people looking to win, and sometimes that win takes a long time to see. I found that I needed the small wins, every day, to keep me focused. I take time each morning, as I get ready for the day, to consider the big challenge I need to solve, the things I need to do and the wins that are possible within my day. I don't have a magic number of goals for each day – some days I need to perform better than others. I simply take what needs to be done and set out to get it done. I aim to focus on the things that build my business and not to get distracted by the things that don't.

Focus on what only you can do

I read about this concept online, although the source now eludes me. As business leaders, we should focus the majority of our time each day on the things that 'only we can do'. It was a very interesting thought for someone who was filling his day trying to get everything done within our business.

The article suggested that if I did not know what 'only I could do', I should ask people in the business to get a valid answer. I remember asking my leadership team this question and was surprised by their answer. I thought it would be something like managing the accounts, delivering digital strategy or closing deals. Instead I was given two primary functions that I didn't spend a lot of my day doing: driving culture and inspiring the team.

Since then, I have slowly begun spending more and more time focusing on these two contributions and have been delegating the work 'others can do' to the rest of my team. It has been fascinating to see that, as I let go of things, other people on the team tend to do the work better than me because it's the work 'only they can do'.

Delegating to others should mean that you spend more time adding value and less time doing stuff. In a world of commoditisation and heavy competition, we need to spend as much time as possible adding value to our service, business and customer.

Get away

You need downtime to let your brain reset. Your brain makes the best decisions when it is not stressed. That's why we often solve problems in the shower.

Make sure you regularly unwind and relax your brain. You will find you will make better decisions in the long run.

Take time to consider, then implement with confidence.

Too many entrepreneurs act quickly, without thinking things through. They do this because they have huge volumes of work to deal with and massive responsibilities that occupy their mind. Given the choice, an entrepreneur would love to spend more time making sure their solution is right. Time simply does not allow it.

I have found that splitting my problem-solving into two parts has helped me make decisions faster and better.

Part One: Gather information

I take the time to read up on the problem as much as possible, before I have to make a decision. The minute I hear about a meeting that has been set to solve a problem, I take time to read everything regarding that problem as soon as possible.

Part Two: Simmer

Then I let this information 'simmer' over time before the meeting. This simmer time has become invaluable to me – it helps me think through things thoroughly, away from time constraints and the pressure to make a call.

As entrepreneurs, we're generally always thinking about the business. Direct your thoughts by reading up on the

FIVE YEAR MARK

problems you need to solve, early on in the decision-making process. Then the thinking time will move into your 'dead' time and not 'work' times.

20

BUILD FOR SALE

In my early twenties, I played drums in a local rock band. I remember spending every cent I owned on drum gear – new cymbals, drums, sticks, microphones, cables, computers, headphones and just about anything that would help me become a better drummer. I saw value in anything that could help me sound better or perform better.

My drum kit was my prized possession and, while others didn't see much in it, it was priceless to me. I never regretted a single cent I spent on that drum kit.

Value is interesting like that – the person considering the value predominantly defines it. What's valuable to some people may not be valuable to others. Some people, like me, would spend a fortune on drums. Others would never see the point.

How do you know what you're building is valuable?

FIVE YEAR MARK

It's a question I have deliberated on for the past few years, trying to understand when a business becomes valuable.

As I thought about it, things came to mind like:

"A business is valuable when its employees are able to support their families and live successful lives."

"A business is valuable when it makes a social impact on the community around it."

"A business is valuable when it has the stability to support its employees though a recession."

While all of these statements are true to an extent, I eventually stumbled across this:

"A valuable business is one that someone would like to buy."

It's the ultimate statement of value, when someone will spend money to own something. Just as the value of my drum kit came from the amount I was willing to spend on it, a business' value comes from what someone would be willing to pay for it.

My objective became to *build for sale*. It wasn't because I wanted to sell; it was because I wanted to build something of value. I began researching what people looked for in a business they were thinking of investing in.

In various conversations with business professionals, I came to realise that there were a few key areas that add considerable value to a business. I set out to include them in ours. These were:

A strong leadership team

I started looking for the best people I could find, inside and outside our team, who had the capacity to grow our business and deliver on its promises.

I quickly found out why this was an important attribute of a valuable business. These leaders took the business to an entirely new level – they contributed more to our success than I could ever have done on my own.

Focusing on building a strong leadership team also helped us to reassess what responsibilities each leader should own, so that our business could operate effectively.

FIVE YEAR MARK

Profitability

Four out of five years have been profitable for us since we started. However, when comparing DigitLab against our industry, I realised we had a lot of room for improvement.

Focusing on being a more profitable business has helped us increase our value as an agency, simply because we have more resources to deliver better work to our clients. We have the strength to make the right decision for our business, instead of chasing the next cash cow.

We have sought to innovate new services and products to stay ahead of our competitors, and we have started focusing our attention on improving under-performing divisions in the business.

Operationally sound

Operations in small businesses are generally less organised as they revolve around the founder's way of doing things. If you are building a business for sale, it becomes highly important to build robust procedures, policy and reporting, to manage the operations of the business well.

Doing this changed our business. I worked with my business coach, Brent "Spillly" Spilkin, to analyse our entire business and develop strong lines of reporting, ensuring that the business was being operated efficiently.

The whole process has helped us understand the business better, reduce anxiety within the team, make better decisions and start to plan more strategically for the future.

By focusing on these three areas alone, we were able to build a more valuable business. Focusing on our business as if it were for sale, helped us see big areas that needed serious work.

We're better for it. We are stronger and more valuable. Building for sale has helped us understand the business and gear it in the right way to manage things more effectively. Although we may never sell the business, we are happy to be a part of a more valuable business vehicle that can and will unlock our vision.

FIVE YEAR MARK

CULTURE

"Customers will never love a company until the employees love it first"
Simon Sinek

MIKE SAUNDERS

› FIVE YEAR MARK

21

KEEP TRACK OF THE SMALL WINS

A few years ago, I did something very stupid. I agreed to go on a hike with a bunch of good mates. I thought it would be a great idea; things in life were very stressful. I felt pretty close to burnout, so I thought a weekend in the Drakensberg would be great, especially with good friends. I just hadn't considered that I was very unfit and hadn't gone on a hike or done any exercise in almost two years. And yet, there I was, signing up for a two-day hike along the steepest hiking terrains in KwaZulu-Natal.

We woke up early on the Saturday morning and drove for two hours to Monk's Cowl, the starting point. We began our hike to Zulu Cave in the cool of the morning, and the start of the hike includes a very steep climb. For many people, it would be a moderately difficult start to the morning. I, however, found the start incredibly tough. Carrying my very unfit and overweight body up the hill turned out to be far harder than I'd initially thought. My legs started to feel like I was climbing Everest and I wondered if I could ever make it to Zulu Cave. My mind was playing serious games with me and I contemplated giving up before I found myself dying of exhaustion in the Drakensberg somewhere. Dramatic, I know, but I felt like I was dying!

To get up that hill, I committed to counting each step and almost congratulating myself each time. It seems crazy, but I needed to keep my focus on each small step that took me up the hill. I eventually made it up, but I am still embarrassed today about how long it took me to get there. I mean, I've heard of children going on this hike. It is, by no means, a tough hike. In my defence, I ended up getting very sick on the hike and was booked off work for two weeks afterwards to try and recover from burnout.

When you're chasing down a dream in business, the big milestones are often very far apart. Like the difference between the bottom of a mountain and the top of it, sometimes we lose sight of the big win at the summit and we get lost in our view of the size of the challenge – it seems like we'll never make it. It's because of these times that I have tried to build a habit of tracking the small wins.

Each project has an end goal, but there are many smaller milestones before we reach it. Each milestone should be celebrated, because this helps to keep people on track, give them hope and keep their perspective.

FIVE YEAR MARK

Celebrating small wins is akin to reaching a viewpoint on a hiking route and looking at the view, reassessing your path and looking at how far you've come. Taking the time to do this will re-energise your team and give them strength for the next few steps.

22

RECRUIT THE RIGHT PEOPLE

People can make or break your business. In our industry and others, the war over talent is growing tougher, especially for small businesses that may not be able to offer great company packages to their staff. It's always a challenge to get people to join the team, which sometimes means that entrepreneurs end up settling for people who will get the job done and not much more. We need to find a way past this, to keep our focus on getting the best people into our team.

In our business we have a four-step process that we use for most of our new hires. This process has served us well in finding great talent.

CV review

This is the most critical part of the process. We make quick judgment calls on the basis of the CV quality. We will have a hit list of qualifications and experience that we are looking for and, if we find these listed in a particular CV, we will shortlist the candidate.

Meet and Greet interview

The first interview with a potential candidate has two primary outcomes for us. We seek to answer two questions: "Can we get along with this person?" and "Does he or she have the capability to do the job at hand?"

During this interview, we make sure that the people who will rely on this person are present so that they are confident in his or her ability. I never attend these interviews, because I am the wrong person at this point. I look for potential in people, so I may favour someone who hasn't got the skills but has untapped potential. This often means hiring people that can't perform in the role quickly.

Prove your worth

We then have a series of tests that candidates take home to complete. These tests will be specific to the role the candidate will play in our business and are used to assess whether or not they are truly as good as they say they are.

This is often the point where many candidates fail, and it has saved us a lot of time, because we don't hire weaker candidates by mistake.

It may sound harsh, but the repercussions are even worse if the person is not competent enough to do their work. It will knock their own self-worth, along with the productivity levels of their manager and those around them.

Culture Fit interview

The final step is a dedicated interview with the CEO. My role in this interview is to dig deeper into their personality. I look for two things: capacity and fit.

In searching for capacity, I look to see how much capacity this person has to grow within our business; what motivates them and whether or not I believe they could stay with us on a long-term basis. We value lasting relationships, so I don't want to hire someone who I don't think we can keep within our business for an extended period of time.

FIVE YEAR MARK

Culture fit is the next aspect I review. I have a host of questions and scenarios that I have developed over time to try and uncover the reality of a person and their character.

It's not always easy but it's worth the time to dig deep into a person's life to see if they will fit into your business. I contemplate the following things:

- Will they complement others in the team and challenge us where we need to be challenged?
- How do they handle conflict?
- Do they see themselves as victims of life or in control of their future?

All of these attributes help me assess whether or not they are a good fit for our culture.

There have been times when I have hired without being sure of a culture fit, and it's never turned out well. I made these appointments because we needed the people and I was under pressure to fill a vacancy. Every time, their impact on our culture has been more expensive than waiting for the right person who would be the right fit.

23

AUTONOMY AND TRUST

I am no stranger to hard work – my parents actively advocated for their children to learn its value. When I was thirteen, my mother proudly announced that she had found me a job working in a restaurant. I was too young to work as a waiter, so I was kept in the back making milkshakes and ensuring dishes were clean. I got used to the idea of working my weekends away and actually quite enjoyed it. I liked the extra cash too, and learnt early on that you need to work hard to earn a living.

I've had an array of jobs since then: I've waited tables, worked behind bars in the UK, been a camp counsellor in South Africa and the USA, managed restaurants, been a sales assistant in a hardware store and a music store. I've taught drums to school kids, been on tour for three months, and I have set up more stages, lighting rigs and sound systems than I care to remember. I've also cleaned toilets, scrubbed floors, and worked my fair share of 22-hour days.

FIVE YEAR MARK

When I scooped my very first job in marketing, I was prepared to put in the extra effort and do the work that needed to be done.

What really shocked me was the irrational tradition of holding people to their lunch hours and working a standard eight-hour day. The incessant clock-watching didn't make sense to me. I once found myself sitting in a doctor's room waiting for an appointment that was running late. I had to leave the appointment before it started, because I had to be back at work by a certain time. It often happened that I wasn't able to go to the doctor when they could see me. As much as I questioned this crazy notion, I was simply told: "that's the way it is". I was an early riser, starting work at 5:30am every morning and working until late at night – but I couldn't have the freedom to use my lunch break at a more convenient time, so that I could actually get something done.

When I started DigitLab, I was a big advocate of flexi-time, allowing staff to choose when they would like to start and finish work, when they would like to use their lunch break, where they would like to work from, and how they would like to plan their day. I offered this freedom to every single employee, regardless of their role in the business, on the simple proviso that you ensure you don't drop any deadlines and get all your work done.

As the business grew, however, it became a little more

difficult to keep to our flexi-time nature. We have had people abuse it, we've employed people for roles requiring them to be available at specific times, and we have sometimes struggled to set meetings with people because they are not in the office. Yet in every situation, we have developed ways of working around these challenges and the business has never suffered because of our flexi-time arrangements.

The upside has been worth it. When people are able to plan their day with a clear understanding of what they need to achieve, they can make decisions that help them be more productive. They can plan personal errands when it least impacts the business, and they may even make the choice to work overtime in places so that they are able to meet their deadlines. This becomes their choice, instead of being forced on them.

The biggest reason I like the flexi-time model has to do with a simple productivity tool we use. We encourage people to find their two most productive hours and to guard them with their life. In my day, it is the first two hours of every day: between 5:30am and 7:30am. Eighty percent of the work I produce each day comes from those early morning work sessions. I am able to focus better, work faster and think more clearly than during any other time of the day. For others in the office, their best two hours lie between 10:00 and 12:00, or between 16:00 and 18:00. Allowing people the freedom to plan their working hours enables them to structure their days around their strengths and choose the hours they are most productive.

This flexi-time model has affected the systems we use to run our business. Our entire business is run virtually, allowing people the option to work from home, from a coffee shop or from their desk. We use cloud-based collaboration tools like Dropbox, Wrike, Google Hangouts, Skype, Google Docs, Facebook at Work and Wordpress. With all these virtual business systems and flexi-time arrangements, you may wonder: Does anyone actually come to the office?

Our office is actually packed most of the day. People only choose to work from home these days when they have too much work and need to focus at home, or because they aren't well and don't want to infect the office with their germs. It's been interesting to see how most people, when presented with virtual office tools and flexi-time opportunities, choose to work at the office. I know I can thank our company culture and communication for this.

People miss the culture and it attracts them back to the office. The office becomes a place where you can 'be at work', while flexi-time arrangements and virtual office tools make it easier for people to be productive at work even when they can't be there.

It is naive, and slightly arrogant, to think that your business objectives are the only thing on your employees' minds every day. They have personal ambitions too, families to take care of, health concerns and a host of other challenges competing for their focus every day. Flexi-time arrangements have allowed us to respect the lives of our employees enough that they return the favour by not letting us down as we chase our dream.

We have always found that respecting our employees first creates a better, faster way for us to build a relationship founded on mutual respect.

//FIVE YEAR MARK

24

#WORKFAMILY

The idea of a work family is not a new one. People spend most of their time at work and there's always a point where their colleagues start to feel a bit like family. Between shared experiences, a family-like relationship and environment is cultivated and grown.

At DigitLab, this concept became a part of our culture in the most incredible way. We didn't communicate the idea of work family; to be honest I had never heard of it before. As it stands today, it does not exist in the dictionary, not even Urban Dictionary. Our team members began posting photos of work online and using the hashtag #workfamily. It caught on quickly and, before long, #workfamily became a conversation that happened inside our business.

People affectionately called out "hashtag work family" whenever they wanted to express gratitude for the rest of the team. It became a groundswell that we felt we had to adopt as a language to describe our family culture at DigitLab.

Implementing a #workfamily culture was simple when we first started. As a small team of less than ten people, it was easy because we all knew each other; we worked in the same space and even started socialising together. As we grew into a bigger team, we started to feel this culture disappear a bit. It got harder to embody our #workfamily culture naturally and we needed to find ways to scale the #workfamily idea.

We realised that we needed to define what we meant by #workfamily. We asked these questions: "What is the feeling we want people to have when they are a part of our team?" "How can we easily tell if someone is being treated as part of the family?"

We sat down and tried to encapsulate what it was, and finally settled on two words:

Value

Value speaks to what resides within a person. Value becomes visible through what and how that person contributes to our business. No matter what role you play, we will always do whatever we can to make sure you know that your ideas and work are valued here.

Appreciation

Appreciation is the verb of value. It's the action that naturally follows when you value someone – you show appreciation. You make it known that people are appreciated for the value they put into the business.

People on your team should always feel valued and appreciated. This is what creates a great working environment and keeps people motivated in their career. With this in mind, we set out to make sure our team felt like family by:

- Listening to their ideas and making sure they are heard;
- Giving credit where it is due. Nobody should ever be so insecure that they feel the need to claim someone else's idea as their own;
- Creating an open door policy for any employee to speak to leaders in the business;
- Allowing people to own their successes and their mistakes;
- Communicating frequently about expectations, successes and concerns; and
- Making sure the right people are in the room to contribute towards overcoming a challenge we are facing.

25

HAVE FUN

You may be serious about your work, but creating and enabling opportunities for fun within your business is imperative for your team. Through fun, you create shared experiences and memories and build a stronger team.

Fun makes the stressful moments easier to handle, by breaking the tension and helping your team to keep a good perspective on what life is about. I remember talking to a new recruit, Serena, a week after she started. She found it absolutely hilarious that the CEO, who was interviewing her, was the same guy she saw humping a vacuum cleaner in a "Harlem Shake" video online. At DigitLab, we are not afraid to get silly sometimes.

Creating the opportunity for fun is an important aspect of your business, for so many reasons. Beyond just teambuilding, your clients will also respond to your opportunities for fun. Trust me, people still talk about our

"Harlem Shake" video and yes, we still have the vacuum cleaner.

It's important not to take yourself too seriously and to enjoy the team you're working with. As a leader, you need to adopt fun yourself if you want your team to enjoy their time with you. On his blog, Jonathan Fields shares these four big side effects of having fun at work (Jonathan Fields, 2016):

- It infects the mood of those you work with, with a similar sense of energy and joy.

- It infuses the entire organisation with energy, making it easier to recruit and keep talented, upbeat employees and build a 'culture' of joy.

- It elevates the product or service you provide from a blip on the radar to a STORY that MUST be passed on with zest, creating a source of evangelistic, organic and free buzz.

- It better inoculates you against competition. As our Creative Director once said: "Happy bees make sweeter honey". The happiness of your people directly relates to the quality of your output as a business.

MIKE SAUNDERS

FIVE YEAR MARK

PERSONAL DEVELOPMENT

"He who has a why to live can bear almost any how"
Fredrick Nietzsche

MIKE SAUNDERS

FIVE YEAR MARK

26

KNOW THYSELF

It was a Thursday morning and I was enjoying breakfast with a group of men I admire and respect, because of the way they approach life and inspire others. Our church pastor, Steve Wimble, had invited us to get together and enjoy a meal.

Steve was taking time out of his schedule to meet with leaders in his church, as a way to not only connect with people, but for them to learn about his heart-driven commitment for our local church. We met casually, once a month, to discuss a wide range of topics – from the practical to the spiritual and everything in-between.

In one of these sessions, Steve shared a great analogy about self-awareness. He described the difference between a Formula One race car and our own cars that we drive every day. The team that looks after the Formula One car knows every inch of that car. They know how to get the most out of it and they have improved its performance in every possible way. My car, on the other hand, receives no special attention, is occasionally serviced and sometimes I'll take it to the carwash. It's no wonder that the Formula One team has a better performing car than me – they know more about the car, its performance, its build, its weaknesses and its potential. All I know is that my car can be relied upon to get me to and from where I need to be every day.

This is what self-awareness is: we all have a brain, a body, a heart and a soul. On the day we are born, we are given the mechanics required to make the most of this life. Learning as much as possible about what makes you unique, strong, weak and able to operate efficiently will be a huge help in your quest to get the most from your individual potential.

If you just want to get from A to B and eke out a simple existence, then you are welcome to skip this chapter. If you are looking to find out more about yourself and what you're capable of, then I hope this chapter helps you to unlock your potential.

Self-awareness is a vital attribute, because it enables us to have a better understanding of ourselves. That empowers us to make changes and build on our areas of strength, while identifying areas that we feel could be improved upon.

There are a number of personality tests you can do to help you better understand different aspects of your personality. These are all valuable tools, but using them in isolation can be quite limiting. Using a single process to learn about yourself is like walking around with rose-tinted sunglasses: everything you see will reflect the colour rose. But if I were to drive through traffic wearing those rose-tinted glasses, I wouldn't be able to differentiate between an orange or red light at a busy intersection. For driving, wearing bronze-tinted glasses would work better, because they highlight green and orange lights more effectively.

Learning to look at ourselves through a number of different lenses enables us to analyse different aspects of our individual characters and personalities.

I'll share a little more about the favourite lenses I use to analyse myself. If you're keen to find out more about them, information is easily found online.

The first is one that I have stood by for many years – I have probably gone the deepest in my reading and application of this lens in my life.

The Enneagram

The Enneagram starts with understanding that each person experiences three centres of intelligence:

Heart

Feeling-based types of people emphasise the heart for positive and negative feelings; empathy and concern for others; romance and devotion. Their focus is on success and relationships, performing up to expectations of the job or other people. Also known as the Emotional Centre. (Enneagram Studies in the Narrative Tradition, 2016)

Head

Thinking-based, head types lead with ideas; gathering information; figuring things out and rational decision-making before acting. Their focus is on creating certainty and safety, or finding multiple options. Also known as the Intellectual Centre. (Enneagram Studies in the Narrative Tradition, 2016)

Body

Body-based types lead with the body for movement, sensate awareness and gut-level knowing. Their focus is on personal security; control; social belonging and taking the right action. Also known as the Instinctual Centre. (Enneagram Studies in the Narrative Tradition, 2016)

FIVE YEAR MARK

The ways in which each centre of intelligence is weighted for you, identifies your unique personality characteristics. Using the Enneagram, there are nine personality types.

One of the ways the Enneagram enlightened me was by showing how I operate under stressful and non-stressful circumstances. It helped me see that generally, I am good at delegating work and trusting people to get things done. But when I am stressed about something, I start to take the project over again. Knowing this has helped me see that my natural reaction to take over a project is actually a stress factor. That's empowered me to start asking a different set of questions when I need to manage a problem.

Instead of asking: "How can I fix this?" I have started asking: "Why is this stressing me out?" Usually, the answer lies in communication, or a lack of it. I don't know how the project is going and I begin to feel stressed by my lack of knowledge, which leads me to assume that something could be going wrong.

When information is missing, the human brain tends to create the worst possible scenario – our imaginations are wild with this.

Instead of trying to take over the project when I feel this way, I now call a meeting or send an email requesting an update on the project at hand. Most often, the news is good and I don't need to get involved. Thanks to the Enneagram,

I have been able to identify an area of stress and manage it more effectively to reduce my workload and my personal stress levels.

Myers Briggs

This is a business favourite. I know many people have taken the Myers Briggs test — I find it as valuable as the next person. My personal journey with Myers Briggs has helped me to better understand team dynamics, and cater for personalities I don't naturally understand.

I usually resort to the Myers Briggs test when I need to deal with interpersonal issues within our business. Knowing that I am an ENFJ personality type helps me to work better with my team, many of whom do not have the same personality type as me.

Myers Briggs categorises people according to their personal preferences and allocates a letter to indicate preference types. The preferences these tests assess are: your favourite world, information, decisions and structure.

Favourite World (E or I)

This depends your preferences — your inner or outer world and whether you are an introvert or an extrovert.

Information (S or N)

Do you prefer to look at information at face value, or are you prone to adding meaning to the information you see?

Decisions (T or F)

Do you lean towards a consistent, logical decision-making process, or are you more concerned with people and the special circumstances that may surround the decision?

Structure (J or P)

Are you a person who prefers decisions to be made for or around you, or are you happy to leave things undecided to allow for new information and options?

StrengthFinders

StrengthFinders, officially known as "The Clifton StrengthsFinder™", measures the presence of 34 talent themes or strengths. Talents are people's naturally recurring patterns of thought, feelings or behaviours that can be productively applied. The more dominant a theme is within a person, the greater the theme's impact on that person's behaviour and performance. (StrengthsTest, 2016)

What I like about this lens for self-awareness is that it focuses on your individual strengths, and not your weaknesses. The process is quite positive and uplifting, whereas with self-awareness exercises we can sometimes start to focus more on our individual weaknesses.

I believe that we should focus on making our strengths stronger and that we should deal with our weaknesses by building a team that has strengths where we are personally weaker. If you get this right, and the people on your team apply the same approach, you will build a strong team that complements each other's strengths and weaknesses.

In doing the strengths assessment, my executive team and I realised that moving me back into a Managing Director role would have me working outside of my strengths. Keeping that in mind, we restructured our leadership team to make sure that everyone on the team was playing to their individual strengths as much as possible.

All three of the methods listed above have free online tests you can do to start the process, but I would encourage you to find a personal or business coach who understands these frameworks to help you engage with them more fully.

FIVE YEAR MARK

Trust network

This last exercise is not a personality test but has been a very valuable process for many people on our team. It throws out questions to your trusted network and gives them the ability to respond honestly. The idea works so well because you tend to take the feedback in a positive way, while the people giving it know you well enough to communicate clearly with you. My leadership coach, Graham Kiggan, in collaboration with my pastor Steve, designed the following exercise that I now call the Trust Network.

Ask five people you trust for feedback on these three questions:

- What do I do well?
- What area in my life can I improve upon?
- Is there anything else you think I should be made aware of?

If you use this tool to gain feedback from your trusted network, you will receive a wealth of insight and wisdom that will help you grow – especially if you choose people who are honest with you.

One last point on self-awareness

Personality tests are great tools, but they are far more valuable for your own self-assessment than for using to analyse others.

Far too often, I see people using their personality type as a guideline for how people should work with them. Placing the responsibility on others to get the best out of us is not the point – we can't excuse our own weaknesses and expect others to change to fit around us.

Self-awareness exercises like these exist to help us improve ourselves, help us to perform better in life and turn our everyday motor vehicle into a Formula One race car.

FIVE YEAR MARK

27

ACT WITH INTEGRITY

How would you solve a problem if no one was looking? Would you take the short cut, cheat the system and put your interests before others? If so, then you may need to check your motives in life because the chances are good that your integrity levels are low.

Integrity lies in making the hard choice to stick to your values, your promises and your moral code. Integrity sets the bar for the way in which you want to get things done. For me, integrity is your ability to live your life as authentically as possible, in every respect.

Integrity lives at the heart of great leaders and becomes the rock that influences and attracts the respect of those they lead.

Integrity builds trust

Trust is one of the greatest assets in every business. It takes time to build and can be lost very quickly. A trust relationship, when founded upon integrity, means that even if you unfortunately let someone down, the trust between you is not broken.

People want to do business with people they trust. They want to know that they can rely on you to deliver, but mostly they want to know they can rely on you for the truth.

Integrity builds reputation

If integrity builds trust in people, then the next natural asset you will build is reputation.

Integrity helps you sleep at night

At one point, I was facing a challenge within our business and was uncertain about my approach. Unsure if I was acting with integrity or not, I ended up losing sleep over the situation. Complex as it was, I deconstructed it and realised that I had done the right thing, but I'd gone about it in the wrong way.

FIVE YEAR MARK

It was the first time I'd worked on a project like this and I'd made some mistakes along the way. I decided to own up to my errors and explain my position. That meeting ended well, because the people I was working with appreciated not only my honesty, but my approach too. We still enjoy a great working relationship today.

When we act without integrity, our lives can become very stressful. We end up behaving differently in front of different groups of people, trying to remember which version of the truth they know, what we can say and what we can't.

When you live and run your business with integrity, you enjoy a higher quality of life, simply because you have nothing to hide and have done things to the best of your ability.

28

BE HUMBLE

We've all experienced a braggart – someone who will happily spend hours telling us how great they are, how wealthy they are and just how much they've achieved.

I'm sure we can all think of at least one person we wish would grab a humility check. We're so annoyed by their own over-grown sense of self-actualisation that they become useless or irritating to us.

Humility is one of the most important values in business. For me, humility allows you to put another person's interests first, and enables you to learn. That's why I like our narrative of "Helping People Win" – you need to be in a position of humility in order to put someone else's interests ahead of your own. It's hard to put another person's win before yours, but it's this thought that lives at the heart of humility.

John Dickson has written a great book, "Humilitas", where he explains that humility is not being a doormat for others or laying aside your ambitions or strengths. Instead, humility is the noble ability to hold your power for the good of others, instead of for personal gain. In "Humilitas", John illustrates examples of leaders throughout history who displayed great humility, showcasing it as a key ingredient for leadership.

Humble leaders – who use their influence and power for the benefit of those they lead – attract people towards themselves, build trust and unlock the potential within those they lead. The case for humility in leadership becomes clear when you consider these points (John Dickson, 2011):

Humility is common sense

- No one is an expert in everything;
- Expertise in one area counts for very little in another; and
- How much you know should remind you of how much you don't know.

Humility is beautiful

- We like great leaders who are humble, but we don't like those who are great and know it;
- Humble leadership shows the character of the person; and
- Humility means looking to help others, and

everyone likes someone who has their best interests at heart.

Humility is generative

- Humility generates new knowledge because we are not afraid to ask questions;
- The proud person leaves a learning engagement with less than the humble person, who actively wants to learn through the engagement; and
- The humble place is the place of growth.

Humility does not mean you need to let go of your dreams, your vision or your ambitions. Humility simply means that we approach those things in a way that doesn't force them onto others. A humble leader chooses the bigger challenge, using their power to inspire and support people towards a goal instead of forcing it upon them.

Humble people appreciate that others may have greater potential to achieve things than they do. They do not see themselves as the answer to a problem. Instead, they acknowledge and use their power and influence to solve a problem, assisted by the people around them.

A humble person will, most likely, show appreciation for the people around them before pointing to his or her own capacities or abilities. A core attribute of a humble leader resides in their ability and commitment to congratulate

FIVE YEAR MARK

people more for their success, than they themselves are congratulated. They do this simply because they pass on the credit to those who helped them get there.

29

LEARN TO TAKE CRITICISM

Learning to take criticism is never easy, but it is necessary for your personal, and business, growth and understanding. We call it constructive criticism, but the success of it lies in its content and its delivery.

Learning to take and work with criticism is an essential survival strategy in business, and it became all too real to me when our team embarked on a very brave exercise in constructive criticism.

At the beginning of 2015, we decided to run a culture exercise to improve our team's ability to deliver and receive constructive criticism. We watched a series of videos from last year's Global Leadership Summit and then planned a simple exercise.

FIVE YEAR MARK

People have blind spots. These are things you think you're great at, but you're actually not. According to Bill Hybels, the average person has 3.4 blind spots they have no idea about. We asked our team to share each other's blind spot through an anonymous platform, so that people would become more aware of the conflicts they sometimes create or cause.

We knew the risks were big. We knew that some people might be offended and some might take joy in writing hundreds of witty 'blind spots' to share around the office. However, the risk of building a team of people who were too polite to help each other grow was even bigger.

We wanted to create a method where people who wanted to grow personally could put themselves in a place to receive constructive criticism, and that's why we made it a voluntary exercise. This went towards our value of "Unlocking Human Potential" as a business, and we felt the team would be mature enough to manage an exercise like it.

We used the blind spot exercise as an element of building our culture and it worked very well. Most people participated and anxiously waited to receive their personal list of blind spots.

On the day we released those lists of blind spots across our business, I received a list of seven. That may have been the company record for the number of blind spots received.

After receiving my blind spot list, it became abundantly clear to me that people need handles to manage the way they deal with conflict. As I found myself facing this list of constructive criticisms, I realised most of my team were in the same place – wondering what to do with this newfound information. I did some research online and sent them this list of collected resources via email, as a way to help. I hope you find it useful in managing the way you receive constructive criticism in the future.

Don't mouth off

Be careful not to start shouting all over the office about the dissatisfaction you feel regarding your criticism. Mouthing off will reveal more about your character than anything the constructive criticism may have done. It's also far more detrimental in the long run. You don't want to run the risk of creating a barrier to future constructive criticism that you may need to grow. Your peers are your greatest assets here, and you should act in a way that shows you are humble enough to accept the criticism.

Determine if you're over-reacting

We call it constructive criticism, and it usually is. But it can possibly feel painful, destabilising and terribly personal. Notice, and acknowledge to yourself, your feelings of hurt, anger, embarrassment, insufficiency, and anything else that arises. Recognise the feelings, label them, and then put them aside so that the noise of those feelings doesn't crowd out your hearing.

The first time I read my blind spots, I battled with a few of them. Once I had reread them a few times, I started to get a better understanding of the tone and perspective of the comment.

Although I could not tell who had written each one, some of my blind spots weren't easy to accept, because they were things I was actively trying to work on. Other blind spots held truths that I needed to change. Some blind spots even pointed at things I have considered in the past and chosen not to change.

Look beyond the delivery

Feedback is hard to give, and the person offering criticism may not be skilled at doing it well. Even if the feedback is poorly delivered, it does not mean it's less valuable or insightful. Avoid confusing the package with the message.

Organise your criticism

Have you received numerous criticisms that actually speak to one thing? I know I did, and it was much easier to start digesting once I realised I only had three issues to deal with, rather than seven.

Take this shorter list to your mentor, a friend you trust, a family member or spouse to get some honest feedback. I did this straight after getting my list and I found two blind spot areas that I could improve upon.

Don't agree or disagree

Use this time to gather the data. After all, constructive criticism is data related to how people see you and, in the workplace, how they work with and alongside you. While constructive criticism is useful and valuable, immediate change is not always required. I would suggest you begin asking how you see yourself in the light of this new data, and then see what questions come to mind. After some time has passed, make a decision on how you want to react.

Some things will be simple and apparent – you will know they need to change. Others may be more complicated, and that's absolutely fine. Allow yourself the time to make a judgment call – there is no reason to rush this journey.

FIVE YEAR MARK

30

HAVE THE TOUGH CONVERSATIONS

At DigitLab, we know, acknowledge and promote the fact that people need to have the difficult conversations. You know the ones I mean – these are the conversations you're putting off, waiting to blow over, hoping they will disappear. In our experience, they never do.

Often, because we try to avoid having these conversations, things amplify or explode, leading to the destruction of a relationship, the derailment of a project or the loss of someone from our team. These conversations cannot be ignored. In fact, as businesspeople, we need to become really good at having them.

It was one of my lowest points of leadership at DigitLab. I was sitting in a room, exhausted after a week-long process of employee annual reviews. I find annual reviews very draining because they involve so much preparation and create a high level of emotional stress for everyone involved.

I also don't believe that they work, but that year we'd chosen to implement them because they were seen as 'best practice'. Annual reviews are a hotbed for creating clashes between employee expectations and business requirements.

The very last employee on our list for the day walked into the room for his review. He's a friend and someone I respect very much, so I thought this would be an easy one. I was so very wrong.

Our conversation moved towards salary expectations and, in my tired state, I began to feel frustrated and angry. My friend, on the other side of the table, picked up on my angst and also began to feel quite angry. It was not the best start to an annual review.

After the only near-shouting match I've ever had at DigitLab, I asked to stop the conversation and restart it. I asked him to put the figure on the table that he believed he should earn. After he did, I was relieved. Our executive team had agreed, a few weeks earlier, to meet that exact salary expectation. There was, after all, nothing to fight about and absolutely nothing needed to be defended.

We had just spent ten minutes arguing about something we both agreed on. The meeting ended well, but I will always remember the beginning of that meeting. Our battle lines were drawn and I handled it badly, moving into a defensive mode, instead of one focused on resolution.

We replaced the annual review process with a highly effective mentoring programme that better suits our unique business requirements. This progamme is far more efficient and helps us to understand our people better, dealing with concerns quickly from both sides of the employer/employee relationship.

Business is full of conversations like this. They are not simple, but they are necessary. Developing your ability to have these tough conversations is a valuable way to spend time. I've had to have my fair share of them and I've learnt their value. Every time I have these conversations, whether with team members, clients or partners, I am reminded that learning to resolve conflict is one of the most valuable skills a leader can have.

I believe that people need to take personal responsibility for resolving any tension they may have between themselves and the people they work with. It is ultimately the responsibility of the person who feels that angst to act on it, and here's why:

Don't create weak links

A team is only as strong as its weakest link. When people avoid the tough conversations, they weaken the link between themselves and others. They then become a weaker link, perhaps even becoming your business' weakest link. Under pressure, weak links break.

Relationships are key

Relationships are often the biggest reasons why people go the extra mile. When you like, trust and believe in your team, your approach to working with them is selfless. You focus on doing the best you can for those around you, and your conversation is more humble and collaborative. Committing to solving grievances will ultimately build trust in your team, while avoiding them usually results in teams being governed by gossip, politics and poor performance.

Look for resolution

There is always more than one side to a story. There are also various versions of the 'truth' and varied perceptions about who is in the wrong. It's always easier to place blame onto someone else and never actually resolve the issue. People often only want to know one side of the story, their side, because it makes them feel justified in their anger. Once the blame has been passed onto someone else, we think our work is done. If you're looking for justification, then yes, your work is done. If you're looking for resolution to gain and build trust, then your work has just begun.

Create opportunities for resolution

By avoiding these conversations, you take an important opportunity away from the people in your team. They are left without a chance to explain, apologise or make sense of their actions. Most often, people who are feeling hurt, angered or isolated in business are merely responding to a miscommunication, ignorance or differing levels of expectation. These are issues that can be easily solved. When left unresolved, however, they can have a highly negative impact on your business culture and employee relationships.

I am in no way a conflict resolution expert, but I can offer some simple tips that have helped me tackle these issues:

Balance time and emotion

There is a delicate balance between time and emotion, when it comes to these conversations. You need to give things time, so that your responses are not driven purely by emotion. However, leaving a potential conflict situation for too long could make it worse.

The magic time for me has always been once I have dealt with my emotions to the point that they don't drive my desired outcome. After that time has elapsed, I am able to lead a conversation towards resolution, regardless of how angry or unhappy I may feel. If people approach me to talk before I reach this point, I tell them that it's simply not the right time because I am unable to think clearly about a resolution. Self-awareness becomes your greatest tool in this regard.

Focus on the problem

To find resolution in a conflict situation, you need to focus on the point of the conflict, and not become distracted by seemingly related factors or circumstances. When dealing with conflict, people often feel a need to build a case behind their cause or against the cause of the other position. It's natural for people to do this and we can't be upset when it happens; but you can't get caught up in it if you're working towards a resolution.

If the focus of the discussion is an operational issue, don't get caught up in personality issues. If the discussion is about how to deal with the consequence of a decision, don't get caught up with why the decision was made. Aim to resolve the issue at hand. If the conversation raises new issues, feel free to deal with these in later conversations, when you are more prepared to tackle them.

Integrity of speech

It's easy to see whether or not you're heading towards a resolution – you'll hear it in the way people speak. When people degrade each other, exaggerate the situation or defer all responsibility, you are headed for trouble. These words show personal vendettas, defensive behaviour and a blame-orientated approach. Above everything, we should always enter difficult conversations with truth and humility. If you don't know the truth, then search for it humbly, through the conversation. If you know the truth, then present it humbly, and be open enough to consider new information.

Questions beat accusations

Emotionally-charged conversations jump quickly to accusations. Accusations get people's defences up and that usually results in retaliation. Instead, do everything you can to rephrase an accusation into a question. It is such a valuable exercise, because it diffuses the tension and enables you to get the bottom of your accusation, eventually enabling you to uncover the truth.

31

DEALING WITH STRESS

I was 24 years old, comfortably enjoying my very first job after graduating from university. I felt like I'd struck it lucky. I was working as the marketing manager for a local school and the work had exceptionally easy targets to meet. I was reaching my weekly targets by every Monday afternoon, and I was forced to take the school holidays as leave. In addition, I had to take the standard fifteen days' leave we're all used to. Collectively, it added up to many days off, and I was earning the best salary I'd ever earned up until then. I thought I had it made – but I could never have been more wrong.

Ten months into my tenure at the school, I leaned back in my chair and started to see little black dots appear in my vision. It was strange for me, because this had never happened before and the black dots wouldn't go away. I called my doctor, Annemie, and explained what was happening. It seemed ridiculous that I was making such a big fuss about a few black dots, but my doctor insisted on seeing me.

After a battery of tests and a very long conversation, Annemie gave me the very sobering news that I was on the edge of a nervous breakdown.

I did not believe her. Nervous breakdowns are for people enduring heavy stress in their lives and I was barely stressed by work; I had lots of leave and life was going so well.

Annemie was gracious with my ignorance as she explained to me that, given my work circumstances, I was most likely feeling a lot of guilt because of how easy I was finding my job. Although it was easy, I was slowly feeling more and more guilty about taking a salary for doing so little in return. That guilt created a build-up of stress that was leading to my first nervous breakdown.

My doctor advised me to find a more challenging job and to make some changes to my life that would help me to manage stress more effectively. That nervous breakdown never did catch up to me, but being near the edge of it changed my view on stress.

Stress is constant

Stress is always present in your life, and it can take on many forms. If you're not stressed at work, something may be creating stress in another area of your life. No matter what, there always seems to be a degree of stress that has become a companion on our journey through life.

Sometimes, stress has served me well. It has fired me up and created the reason for me to push through a tough situation.

In 2004, I started my first business. ShowCore was a technical production company that helped event managers by looking after sound, lighting, staging and security at big events. I was living at home, earning R2 000 a month, and the rest of life was very comfortable. I didn't need ShowCore to work because my life was basically stress-free. Of course, you've already guessed that ShowCore lasted just seven months and ended rather unceremoniously.

A few years later in 2010, I started my third business. I had just been retrenched and I had a family to look after – I had to make this work. I put my head down, focused and got through the first year of successfully running my own consultancy.

The stress from my circumstances forced me to focus and to make it work. A certain amount of stress in life is inevitable and not necessarily a bad thing. Sometimes, stress is necessary to inspire or force us to make changes we need. Perhaps we may need to put in more work to meet a deadline, implement changes to our lifestyle or make a career change. Stress will always be there, and too much will surely break us down. That's why we need to develop ways to manage it successfully in life.

While looking towards managing stress in my own life, I have found a number of very useful tools and frameworks to help me deal with the challenges I'm facing. They are not original concepts but, collectively, they have really helped so I'll share them here.

But first, we need to differentiate between two very particular types of stress – I call them *workload stress* and *emotional stress*. It's important to identify which type of stress you are dealing with, because the solution for each is often very different.

Workload stress

Managing a stressful workload is tough, especially when deadlines are tight and expectations are large. You will know when you're dealing with this stress because you'll see it immediately. Your diary will be too full, your inbox will feel out of control, and you will begin to panic. You'll start to feel overwhelmed, not knowing how to tackle the workload ahead of you.

This is my favourite type of stress, because it's the easiest to control and manage. It's caused entirely by mismanaging your resources and commitments. By devoting an hour or two to planning, you are usually able to define what needs to be done to solve the issues you're faced with.

I apply this process on a continuous basis to manage work stress:

Merge all lists

This is wisdom from David Allen's "Getting Things Done" (GTD) process. It's difficult to manage a big workload when you have your tasks scattered all across separate lists. It's also more difficult to assess the size of your workload and to see your progress as you start ticking things off the lists. I start by making sure I have all my tasks in one place.

GTD is a wonderful methodology that helps you to efficiently and effectively deal with your workload. I would highly recommend you do some reading on this if you haven't already.

I have used a number of applications in the past to help me manage this. "Things", the task management mobile application, was a great help getting me started with GTD methodology.

Prioritise and defer

Once your list is complete, start prioritising the work. I use a simple method to prioritise my lists – I split them into these categories:

- Work I promised someone I would complete;
- Work only I can do, that is holding up the progress of other work;
- Work other people can do that I am holding onto;
- Work I committed to that isn't urgent; and
- Work that does not help me achieve my goals.

Once I understand the task in terms of these categories, I start writing emails and communicating to people how I plan to tackle the work ahead.

To people I have made promises to, and for the work only I can do, I email them to remind them I'm committed to the project and I provide them with a brief update on when they can expect the work from me. This gives them the confidence that I am still able to deliver, and offers them an opportunity to confirm that the delivery deadlines are right. This helps to drive clarity into the project.

The work that others can do gets delegated to people who have the skills and capacity to help. I then schedule delivery dates with these people to ensure the expectations I have are being met.

The work I have committed to but don't consider urgent, I delay or defer. I pick a time when I can get to the work and reschedule the work for then. My favourite application to help me with this is Gmail – specifically the Inbox extension to their email app. The 'sleep' function on this extension enables me to completely clear emails out of my inbox and defer important but non-urgent emails until a later date.

In working with this last category, it's important to set expectations with the people relying on you. I can give you two examples where I have done this in life and work.

Firstly, I set an expectation inside my business that I would not be responding immediately to any email. If something important came up, people were to WhatsApp me and I would treat that as urgent. Email was getting me down and I found myself being tied to my inbox all day. When I made this call, I promised that I would set aside time every two to three days to clear my inbox of every email. This meant that everyone could trust that they would get a reply, but they also knew that if they needed me urgently, they could find me on WhatsApp. After setting this expectation, I became three times more productive on a day-to-day basis. It won't work for everyone because the nature of his or her work may be different from mine.

The second expectation I set was with everyone in my personal life that sends me an invoice. I state clearly that I handle all invoices and payments once a month, on the same day, every month. This means that they know when they will get paid, and I turn one part of my personal life into something that I deal with every month at a set time.

Finally, for the work that isn't important, I write short, polite emails to the relevant people, letting them know that I cannot help them with this work. The sooner you do this, the less guilt you will feel because they are still relying on you.

Set aside time

When it comes to work I have promised delivery on, that only I can do, and that is important to meeting our strategic goals, I plan the time into my diary.

Every fifteen-minute segment of my day is planned out, and I treat the time I need to do work with equal importance as sitting in a meeting. If you ask for a meeting when I have blocked out time to do work, then I am not available for that meeting.

We need to accept that if we don't set the time aside to do work, then it will always become a stressor to us, as we try to find the time to get it done. We must take control of our time.

Apply discipline

Finally, we need to be disciplined in getting the work done within the timeframes we set. As I started planning work into my diary, I very quickly become booked up for weeks at a time. People asking for meetings often had to wait a long time to meet with me. It was important that when their appointment came around, I did not postpone the meeting because I was not disciplined enough to get the work done within the time that I had set aside for it.

People should never pay the price for our own lack of discipline, especially if they are polite enough to respect the terms of our diary.

One of the best ways I have found to make discipline easier is to identify the best time of day to tackle the big work I need to get done. Every person has a sweet spot in the day, where they can be the most focused and get through the most work. Our Creative Director finds this time in the evenings, whereas I find the mornings to be better. That's why I wake up as early as possible to get through the workload on my plate. Once you've identified this time zone, start to protect it and try not to accept meetings during this time. Using it every day to get through your task list is the most valuable use of that time.

Emotional stress

Emotional stress is tough to identify. It's not as easy to see as workload stress and, very often, it can be masked by workload stress. Emotional stress starts to run your body down, and it hinders your brain in producing the chemicals you need to think clearly and operate efficiently.

Emotional stress, if not managed properly, often puts people in hospital and needs a lot more attention than workload stress to manage.

In dealing with emotional stress, I have learnt a number of lessons:

Manage your health

Back in Annemie's consulting room, she explained that the human body, when looked after correctly, can handle higher stress levels. When you're working with a body that's not operating at optimal levels, things start to fall apart. Her advice to me was simple: eat well, sleep enough and exercise.

I am, however, a legendary comfort eater who far prefers watching a movie to going for a run. My idea of relaxing is not pushing my heart rate beyond 120 beats per minute; it usually involves friends, family and food. This advice was going to be easier to hear than apply.

I started with sleep – I figured I could handle that. I made getting seven and a half hours' sleep a night a priority. I went to bed earlier so that I could still rise early to tackle my morning workload. I found it worked wonders. It felt like my mind was clearer after a good night's sleep.

These days, I also choose to start my days later when I am feeling a bit run down. I find if I allow myself a few days of eight or nine hours' sleep, my body usually recovers from illness quite quickly.

Next on the list was eating correctly. It took me ages to find a diet that worked for me, and my weight fluctuated dramatically over ten years. I have now found a great diet, which I won't share because it works for me – it may not work for you. My advice to you is to do the research and find out what suits you. Discovering the right diet has helped me lose weight and binge less on the wrong foods. The biggest win, however, was that I found my emotional state was more constant. I used to eat a lot of sugar so I went through spikes of energy, followed by big dips of lethargy. During the dips, I was often grumpy and found I dealt with sensitive issues badly. It was a funny realisation when Stacey told me that my mood is directly linked to my stomach.

Finally, exercise. It took a long time to get into a decent exercise regime. Thanks to a crazy travel schedule, falling asleep on planes and being exposed to many germs in different transport modes and countries, I found it very difficult to exercise properly without getting sick. I found it very frustrating to start exercising, only to be off sick again in two weeks.

If you suffer from a similar challenge to this, I would advise the following:

- Take it slow. Don't over-exert your body at first. Your heart is getting used to the fact that it can operate higher than 120 beats per minute.
- Do check-ups with a doctor or health expert. I found a chiropractor very helpful because I carry stress in my back. She helped me design an exercise regime that supported my back more effectively.
- Track your progress – you'll need to know you're improving to stay motivated, when the honeymoon phase disappears.

I can honestly say that learning to eat well, sleep enough

and exercise has made me a better leader. I have more capacity to deal with stress than I used to have, and that makes me a stronger person that people can lean on and trust. It has been worth all the hard work finding my groove in this regard.

The "balanced life" myth

Many people may not agree with me here. Most people believe that leading a balanced life is the best way to manage stress. I have come to realise that it is not.

When people speak about balance they use phrases like "it's all about balance" – but I have learnt that the world presents a subtle challenge that we have all subscribed to. Balance in life has become being the best parent, the best employee, the best leader, the best athlete and the healthiest person ever. The idea of a balanced life has been tainted with the challenge to be perfect at everything. Worst of all, it's creating a generation of guilt-ridden people trying to keep up in an ever-increasingly fast-paced world.

I approach it slightly differently. My approach is to accept that I have a limited resource: time. If I had all the time in the world, I could be the best parent, the best leader, the best musician and the best athlete I could possibly be. Every successful person has chosen to spend their time on a particular aspect of life and they have seen the returns for their work. All too often though, when people are extremely successful in one area of their life, they have tales of disaster for other areas.

I spent so much time getting my business off the ground that I unknowingly neglected my wife. While divorce is rarely one person's fault, I am convinced that stealing time from my marriage to focus on work was a big reason why my first marriage ended in divorce. A success in one area of my life led to failure in another.

Nowadays, I don't aim for a balanced life. I now have priorities that I know are important to me. Those priorities include my family, business, church and health, and they are all competing for my time. I ask myself a simple question:

"What am I willing to steal time from to succeed in this area?"

For example, I made a decision to steal mornings from my family because I leave early for work. It's my most productive work time and, by focusing this time completely on work, I very rarely have to work past 18:00 on a weekday.

I then steal evenings from work to focus on my family. I cook dinner, catch up with my wife, visit family and occasionally attend a church function.

I steal Thursday afternoons from work to spend time with my son. Divorce makes parenting harder and I don't see my son as much as I would like to. It was an easy decision to choose stealing from work so that I could prioritise time with Zac.

In both cases, the priority being stolen from could do with my attention. There is always more to do, more to achieve and more to attend to – that will never change. The trick is deciding if something is worth stealing from somewhere else. Is it that important?

I find this approach helps me carry less guilt because I am being forced to make decisions based on what's important to me. Using the word 'steal' helps me see the negative impact of the choice before I make the decision. I can then come up with a plan to return the time if I feel I should.

The question of "What am I willing to steal time from to succeed in this area?" has become more valuable to me than chasing the dream of a balanced life.

Find what restores you

Too many of us arrive at work on Monday, having had a great weekend but still feeling exhausted. We often get home after work to a barrage of household chores and pass out on the couch in front of the television after a few hours.

It's not a constructive or wise use of our downtime. We're choosing to do something easy, instead of doing what is good for us.

It's easy to crash on the couch in front of the television, but I have found that sitting outside on our patio engaged in a conversation with Stacey is a much better way to restore my energy levels. I often leave these random conversations feeling relaxed and optimistic. Natasha, now our Head of Editorial, is a fanatical runner and she often speaks about her running pursuits as a way to recharge her energy levels. She often feels tired and grumpy if she goes without running for long periods of time.

The lesson here is that we should try and understand what recharges our batteries and restores our soul. Then, we should begin to use as much of our downtime as possible to do those things. Often, it's not about taking a lot of time off, but rather choosing to do the right things with the time we have.

Is this a problem or a tension?

This little piece of wisdom comes directly from leadership expert, Andy Stanley. In a presentation he gave,

Andy highlighted the idea that we should look at the challenges ahead of us, to understand if they are tensions or problems.

Problems can be solved. Once solved, the problem goes away. A problem is short-term and can be eradicated with a solution.

Tensions are a bit more complicated. They often can't be solved and we need to find ways to manage them, so that they produce the least amount of stress in our lives.

It's important to differentiate a problem from a tension, or else we may let problems fester, or stress ourselves out by trying to solve a tension.

Within our business, there is a constant tension to achieve the levels of excellence we expect from our team. It's always there and cannot be solved. Once we reach one level of excellence, we raise the bar, and work towards the next level. We will always look towards the next level in our search for excellence. Therefore, excellence is a tension in our business that we must learn to manage. It's not a problem we can solve.

But, when one of our team members has too much work to do, and it is clear they need help, that means we have a problem. The solution is simple – hire someone to help them.

Accepting something as a tension we need to manage in life helps us deal with it better and limits its negative impact on us.

Outsource the accountability

Dr Henry Cloud gave an excellent example of outsourcing accountability in a talk I saw him present. He said that he was battling to prioritise exercise in his life, even though he knew it was important and he wanted to get his exercise plan on track. He kept finding, however, that he was just too busy to manage it. His solution?

He hired a personal trainer who managed it for him. The personal trainer planned the exercise sessions, held him accountable on the days of his training and ultimately helped him get back on track.

I found this to be great advice. I tried the personal trainer example almost immediately and it helped me so much towards sorting my health out. Since then, I have also outsourced other aspects of my life to people. I asked my business coach to hold me accountable to meeting my strategic goals; I enrolled in vocal coaching to improve my singing ability; and I hired an editor for this book before it was complete, which held me accountable to finishing it on time.

Outsourcing your accountability to coaches, friends, mentors and consultants can be a great way to achieve the things you know are important but are struggling to prioritise. The people you outsource your accountability to can, and will, help you to achieve the things you hope to.

FIVE YEAR MARK

32

EGGS IN ONE BASKET

When I started my journey as an entrepreneur, I committed fully by promptly initiating three business projects simultaneously. The first was DigitLab; the second was joining a futurist consulting firm called TomorrowToday and the third was a Wordpress website hosting business.

Each of these businesses interested me deeply and I was excited about them every single day. They all seemed to work so well together, and in each business I got to work alongside great business partners. Over time though, it became more and more apparent that my split focus across three businesses meant that they all succeeded a little, but never a lot.

I worked in the DigitLab office every day, so that naturally got a lot of my time and attention. TomorrowToday would book my time for consulting events and presentations, so that was relatively easy to manage at the beginning. My hosting business was the first business to fall apart. My business partner saw it before I did, and it took up too much time for the returns we were receiving. After a good, but difficult, conversation, we decided to shut it down and pursue other ventures. In my case, it meant a process of refocusing.

It was the first time I realised just how strongly you need to focus on your business to make it successful. Either you must provide that focus, or you need to hire someone to do it. Whichever way it works for your business, you need a focused individual who nurtures your start-up company, or else it will fall apart.

Then came the next moment of truth. In 2014, I realised that I needed to make a decision. Should I pursue a professional consulting career with TomorrowToday or should I commit completely to running DigitLab full-time? While both were performing well, I was struggling to attend to everything each business needed or demanded from me. After much deliberation, I made the decision to leave TomorrowToday and to focus my attention on unlocking the DigitLab vision.

In April of 2014, I wrote this blog post to announce my resignation from TomorrowToday:

> *"It's hard to measure a life – I don't think life should only be measured by the fun you've had or how much you enjoy:*

FIVE YEAR MARK

sometimes it is hard to take hold of the things that really matter. I don't think it should be measured by the size of your wallet — I know plenty of people who have wasted their lives chasing money, having lost everything in the process. I also don't think life can be measured by a single attribute. Life is far more beautiful and intricate than that — life is more like a diverse tapestry, instead of a colourful piece of cardboard.

In the movie "The Bucket List", Morgan Freeman says that you should measure your life by those who measure theirs against yours. I love this quote. It reminds me that people mark your life, in good ways and bad. They impact you, challenge you, inspire you, mentor you and basically shape the person you become.

Great people surround me. That's why I count myself blessed. My son is the light of my life; my wife is truly the most exquisite person I have met; DigitLab is packed full of the most dedicated and talented people and TomorrowToday is the wisest counsel I have been privileged to sharpen my mind against.

So what's the hard decision?

At the beginning of the year, it became clear that my time working alongside the TomorrowToday team was coming to a close (at least for a season). It was sparked by a growing realisation that I needed to be more available for my family and the team at DigitLab. These aspects of my life have grown and were demanding more of my attention. I'm glad they've grown, but it was hard to make the decision to step away from the most astute team of people I have ever worked with.

Keith Coats has been my leadership mentor and guide through many of the toughest leadership challenges I have ever faced. Graeme Codrington has this incredible ability to sharpen a person's thinking in every circumstance and has been the inspiration behind many tough conversations I have been in. Vicky has been the never-ending support and Jude, always bringing calm and fun to every situation.

Above all, they are my friends. We have nursed each other's failures and celebrated our success. We have spent many evenings around the fireplace solving the world's problems and even more time building into each other. These are people I would measure my life against.

As of the 1st April 2014, I am no longer a Partner at TomorrowToday. I will remain an Associate and will be called upon to deliver work to TomorrowToday clients that I am working with. No existing client projects will be jeopardised.

As I step into DigitLab in a full-time capacity, I am very excited to realise new opportunities in my capacity as CEO. Watch this space, because DigitLab is still bent on making a massive difference in the Digital Marketing arena."

FIVE YEAR MARK

The day after this blog post was published, I went into DigitLab as a full-time, completely focused, CEO for one business. All of my attention has been dedicated to unlocking the DigitLab dream and we have come a long way since then. Choosing to focus my attention on one business was one of the best decisions I have made to date. It is abundantly clear that your ability to provide leadership to a team is directly linked to your focus on and commitment to that team.

There is something great about people knowing you need to make this work as much as they do. Your business partners will appreciate your focus, your employees will appreciate it and your customers will feel the difference.

I have often spoken with entrepreneurs who talk about their business partner's lack of focus on their business. It is, almost always, because of another business venture in their partner's life that they feel is distracting them from their current role in the business. I've seen this breed dissention that often does not get dealt with, because of the awkwardness of the conversation. It may not break a partnership, but it certainly will decrease the levels of trust in that partnership.

I highly recommend that entrepreneurs focus their time and energy on the one thing they know they can turn into brilliant work. Focus your attention and provide good leadership for your team and your customers. They will all thank you for it in the long run.

If you are a serial entrepreneur, make sure you hire and partner with people who will provide that commitment and leadership to your team. If you are not able to lead the team in that way, make sure someone is there who can and will.

If you can't have all your eggs in one basket, make sure someone does.

FIVE YEAR MARK

THE NEXT FIVE

"Even if you're on the right track, you'll get run over if you just sit there"
Will Rogers

MIKE SAUNDERS

33

BE WILLING TO CHANGE

It has become very clear to me that the tactics and strategies we used to get to our Five Year Mark won't take us to the Ten Year Mark.

Writing this book has been a wonderful growth experience as it's forced me to review the last five years, to see what's worked and what hasn't. The entire experience has brought with it a number of truths that we need to return to our business. It has also highlighted that some of our thinking needs to mature and grow, as we step up to an even greater challenge.

That challenge will not be leaning on what we know, but rather reassessing our dream in the context of this ever-changing world, while gearing our business differently to achieve what we set out to do. Every person within our business will be faced with the decision to grow, to scale their capacity and to unlock their leadership potential at DigitLab.

We need to be willing to change our approach to suit a bigger vision and a new digital world, while keeping in mind the core lessons and stories that got us to this point.

FIVE YEAR MARK

34

DREAM BIG…AGAIN

Starting DigitLab was part of a simple dream: to work for myself and to lead a great team of people. Over the last five years, this has been my honour and my privilege. It's some of the most fulfilling work I've ever done and I enjoy every single minute of it.

I started reading David Novak's most recent book, "Taking People with You", and was challenged by his concept of dreaming big. David, Executive Chairman of YUM! Brands, suggests that we need to take our dream, halve the time frame and double the size. Doing this makes us think about the dream differently. It causes us to think more creatively and strategically about how we would achieve the new goal.

That's what we're busy doing at DigitLab. Our entire business has begun to look at our future. We look for the opportunities to unlock our potential by doubling the size and halving the time frame of a seriously big goal.

David suggests that when your dream is big enough, you will begin attracting the people who have that capacity to unlock the dream. Our team is the best team to do that, and we're attracting more people like this to our door. I am more excited about our existing leadership and the way their excitement for our business is growing even more, because of the size of our dream.

Here's to the next five years, as we attempt to unlock another dream. I look forward to seeing you again at *The Ten Year Mark*.

ABOUT THE AUTHOR

Mike Saunders is the CEO of DigitLab, husband to Stacey and father to Zac. He's an entrepreneur who exists to equip leaders toward unlocking the potential within people.

An internationally acclaimed speaker, Mike has had the privilege of working with some of the world's most prestigious organisations including Vodafone, IBM, Microsoft, KPMG, Norton Rose, Mr Price, Toyota and Exxaro. Along with his experience in business, Mike has also contributed to leadership programmes for the Gordon Institute of Business (GIBS) and lectured at the VEGA School of Branding.

In 2014, Mike won the Special Award for Outstanding Contribution to Social Media at the New Generation Social and Digital Media Awards. As an entrepreneur and businessman, Mike has built DigitLab into one of South Africa's premier digital marketing companies. He sits on the International Advisory board of the Internet of Things Asia Conference and on the VEGA School of Branding Advisory Council. He is the founder of Digital Swarm, an event series aimed at accelerating the digital industry.

Visit www.mikesaunders.com or follow @mikeasaunders on Twitter or Instagram.

MIKE SAUNDERS

ABOUT DIGITLAB

We are a digital marketing agency that is fascinated with the ways people are influenced by and enchanted with technology.

Our aim in life is to help people win: to help clients win, our employees win and our partners win. We are obsessed with this – their win is our win and we spend every minute making this happen.

Working with local and international businesses, we have proven that we have the diversity to launch a start-up and market an international consumer brand.

We are digital at heart, creative in spirit and strategic in mind.

We are DigitLab.

Visit www.digitlab.co.za or follow @DigitLabSA on Twitter or Instagram

FIVE YEAR MARK

THIS ACTUALLY HAPPENED

I was asked to speak at a conference in an African city. The main challenge was managing the flights and conference timing to be home by Saturday morning so that I could see my son Zac for the weekend. I spoke to the client and she said, "it would be tight, but we could do it". I had no idea at the time that my client is closely connected with the government, which was driving the initiative for the conference. Essentially, I was their guest. Let me share it with you as I lived it.

Upon arriving in the country, I am fast-tracked through passport control and the government gives me a personal driver from the state. Equipped with sirens and extreme driving skills, the driver introduces himself as Jones – Mr Jones.

The trip to the hotel is fairly uneventful, with Jones making the most of his ABS breaking, power steering and police siren.

The night of the event, I am speaking from 18:30 to 19:15 and then we have a 15-minute question session. All goes well and I am on my way out of the venue a few minutes late. No one seems stressed – they will make the time up on the road.

We leave just before 20:00 and need to get to the airport for a 22:00 international flight back to Johannesburg. The traffic is fairly clear for a few kilometres. Mr Jones drives like he's in a car chase scene involving Vin Diesel.

I decide it's a good idea to buckle up.

We hit traffic. Lots of traffic. Five lanes of traffic on a three-lane 'highway'. Then join an official police convoy and push and wind our way through traffic. Crash into one car as we swerve in a lane and keep going. No big deal.

I am asked to call the state personnel at the airport. I get told to speak to a guy called Prof. I tell Prof that I'm on my way and ask him to meet me when I get dropped off. He says that's fine. He'll call me back.

Prof calls back and says something that I don't understand. He realises I'm an idiotic foreigner and hangs up. He calls Mr Jones. Jones hangs up and tells me they're going to delay the flight so I can get on board. I kid you not!

Apparently, it helps when you're a guest of the government.

I am now in the back of the car about to throw up from all the swerving while typing. I sneeze. Jones comes out of driving frenzy to say 'I'm sorry'. I think he meant 'bless you'. Either that or he's sorry there's sneeze debris all over the back of his seat. The guy must have all his senses on high alert.

Time: 20:53. Roads clear...ish. Resembling three lanes of traffic again, back to Vin Diesel car chase scene. Sirens on. Lights spinning on the cop vehicles we're in convoy with.

20:56. Traffic slows down, our convoy does not. All non-official convoy members dive out of the way of the convoy at the first sign of streetlights. We do not.

Mr Jones picks up a ringing cellphone. This man is either gifted or insane. I'm going with gifted. Makes me feel safer. Prof is on the phone asking how close we are. Jones replies. Close! Hangs up and gets back into gifted driving mode.

21:00. Arriving at the airport. Traffic slows, and so do we, but not before a small negotiation with a cement truck.

21:05. Can see the entrance but a small army of vehicles stands between us. Mr Jones is up to the task. Sirens on. Didn't help much.

21:08. Call Prof to say I'm close. He's waiting outside. These guys are on form.

At this point, I think I'm enjoying this too much. Prof finds me in the traffic and he decides we should run the last hundred metres for fun, I guess. I bid Jones farewell and we hit the road. I get to the check-in queue that we bypass by just walking to the front, and Prof hands them my passport and ticket. Without batting an eyelid, they let me in and process my boarding pass.

Some guy approaches me in the airport and Prof's boss (I think) launches into a very aggressive verbal attack on the man in front of me. I have no idea what the problem is but he is clearly out of line. I then race through all the queues, passport control and security and quickly walk toward my plane.

21:40. Arrive at the boarding gate and immediately board the plane, which wasn't delayed, and I finally feel relief that I'm heading home and won't be spending the night on a cold bench in the airport.

Even better news is that I will see Zac in the morning. I wonder if he knows that the government of this wonderful country did everything they could to get me home to see him.

All I can say is thanks for the ride of a lifetime!

REFERENCES

702, 2016. The state of entrepreneurship in South Africa. [ONLINE] Available at: http://702.co.za/articles/4179/the-state-of-entrepreneurship-in-south-africa. [Accessed 31 August 2016].

Dickson, John, 2011. Humilitas: A lost key to life, love, and leadership. Zondervan.

Enneagram Studies in the Narrative Tradition, 2016. Enneagram Types. [ONLINE] Available at: https://www.enneagramworldwide.com/tour-the-nine-types/. [Accessed 01 September 2016].

Fields, Jonathan, 2016. Fun money: Why having fun is great for business. [ONLINE] Available at: http://www.jonathanfields.com/the-business-power-of-fun/. [Accessed 22 September 2016].

Harvard Business Review, 2016. Candor, criticism, teamwork. [ONLINE] Available at: https://hbr.org/2012/01/candor-criticism-teamwork. [Accessed 01 September 2016].

Wikipedia. 2016. Two-factor theory - Wikipedia. [ONLINE] Available at: https://en.wikipedia.org/wiki/Two-factor_theory. [Accessed 19 October 2016].

Harvard Business Review, 2016. How to deal with critics. [ONLINE] Available at: https://hbr.org/2012/01/how-to-deal-with-critics. [Accessed 01 September 2016].

Harvard Business Review, 2016. How to handle surprise criticism. [ONLINE] Available at: https://hbr.org/2010/09/how-to-handle-surprise-critici. [Accessed 01 September 2016].

Harvard Business Review, 2016. How to handle negative feedback. [ONLINE] Available at: https://hbr.org/2015/08/how-to-handle-negative-feedback. [Accessed 01 September 2016].

IMDb, 2016. Maggie Carpenter (Character) – Quotes. [ONLINE] Available at: http://www.imdb.com/character/ch0012008/quotes. [Accessed 31 August 2016].

News24 - Breaking News, 2016. Challenges facing young entrepreneurs in South Africa. [ONLINE] Available at: http://www.news24.com/MyNews24/Challenges-Facing-Young-Entrepreneurs-in-South-Africa-20140929. [Accessed 31 August 2016].

Novak, David, 2013. Taking people with you: The only way to make big things happen. Portfolio.

Sowetan LIVE, 2016. Small businesses failure rate high. [ONLINE] Available at: http://www.sowetanlive.co.za/news/business-news/2013/05/16/small-businesses-failure-rate-high. [Accessed 31 August 2016].

StrengthsTest, 2016. StrengthsFinder List – the 34 talent themes. [ONLINE] Available at: http://www.strengthstest.com/strengths-finder-themes. [Accessed 01 September 2016].

FIVE YEAR MARK

MIKE SAUNDERS

www.ingramcontent.com/pod-product-compliance
Lightning Source LLC
Chambersburg PA
CBHW070315190526
45169CB00005B/1630